Shaping the Next Generation

A publication of The Ohio State University
Foreign Language Publications Office

*Produced with funding from the United States-Japan Foundation
and The National Foreign Language Resource Center
The Ohio State University*

Ohio State University Foreign Language Publications Office

    Executive Director, Galal L. R. Walker
    Editor, Christopher W. Antonsen
    Manager, Ami C. Chitwood
    Graphic Designer, Dan O'Dair
    Copy Editor, Rachel S. Besen

Shaping the Next Generation

Papers from the Conference on National Strategic Assessment of Japanese Language Education

University of Maryland at College Park

1995

Edited by J. Marshall Unger

Published in cooperation with
The Ohio State University National Foreign Language Resource Center and
The OSU Foreign Language Publications Office
Columbus, Ohio

1997

© 1997 by The Ohio State University Foreign Language Publications Office, all rights reserved

This volume prepared by

National Foreign Language Resource Center
The Ohio State University
276 Cunz Hall
1841 Millikin Road
Columbus, Ohio 43210

614-292-4361 • fax: 614-292-2682
www.cohums.ohio-state.edu/flc/

Library of Congress Cataloging-in-Publication Data
Conference on National Strategic Assessment of Japanese Language Education
(1995: University of Maryland at College Park)
Shaping the next generation: papers from the Conference on National Strategic Assessment of Japanese Language Education: University of Maryland at College Park, 1995 / edited by J. Marshall Unger.
p. cm.
ISBN 0-87415-332-8 (alk. paper)
1. Japanese language—Study and teaching—United States—Congresses. I. Unger, J. Marshall.
PL520.U5C66 1995
495.6'8'007073—dc21

Manufactured in the United States of America
Printed and bound by Cushing-Malloy, Inc., Ann Arbor, Michigan

ISBN 0-87415-332-8

Contents

Foreword vii
J. Marshall Unger

Policy Issues in Foreign Language and Study Abroad 1
Richard Brecht and Ronald Walton

Between the Idea and the Reality 17
Chris Brockett

**Shaping The Next Generation: A Look at
Teacher Training** 27
Eleanor H. Jorden

**Curriculum Design: Teaching Japanese in
the Humanities** 37
Emiko Konomi

Who Owns The Japanese Language Curriculum? 47
Shigeru Miyagawa

Shaping Curriculum: Transparency of Curriculum 57
Mari Noda

Getting Learners on The Way 77
Charles Quinn, Jr.

Japanese Language Teaching Without Teaching Context 93
Masakazu Watabe

Foreword

The eight papers in this volume are the fruits of a conference held at the University of Maryland at College Park in April 1995. Emiko Konomi, then Assistant Professor of Japanese in the Department of Hebrew and East Asian Languages and Literatures, of which I was Chair, organized the conference with funding from the United States-Japan Foundation, which has also made the publication of this volume possible. My thanks to her for having assembled a truly outstanding group of leaders in the field; their thoughtfulness and their skill in identifying the essential issues of Japanese language pedagogy will, I am sure, become only apparent to readers in the years ahead.

In many ways, the inspiration for this conference came from the late Ronald Walton, who was both Associate Professor of Chinese at Maryland and Deputy Director of the National Foreign Language Center in Washington, D.C. Ron was one of the most imaginative and influential thinkers in foreign language education in the United States; though a specialist in Chinese, his concerns spanned all the "less commonly taught languages." He and Richard Brecht, Professor of Russian at Maryland and another pillar of the NFLC, were the driving forces behind the Second-Language Learning initiative of Maryland's College of Arts and Humanities, of which this conference was a part. Ron had a knack for distilling the insights he gleaned from his eclectic reading, his countless interactions with teachers and administrators, and his experiences with students into simple but powerful words that made people think. In Ron's memory, Richard and I have decided to substitute a paper he co-authored with Ron that elaborates on the themes of Richard's original presentation. Although not specifically about Japanese, it raises the important issue of study abroad in the transition from other-directed to self-directed learning and introduces the pathbreaking research of Brecht, Davidson, and Ginsberg (see note 2), which should be must-reading for everyone concerned with less commonly taught languages.

J. Marshall Unger
Columbus, Ohio
July, 1997

POLICY ISSUES IN FOREIGN LANGUAGE AND STUDY ABROAD

Richard D. Brecht and
A. Ronald Walton

World developments in the past several years have resulted in significantly greater value being placed in the United States on exchanges and study abroad (SA). The SA approach to international education as a long-term response to national security and economic competitiveness has provoked a series of legislative acts that, building upon the proven effect of the Fulbright program, will send many more Americans abroad than ever before.[1]

While the role of exchanges and SA has almost universal acceptance as a proper vehicle to promote international understanding as well as a real and disciplinary expertise, a major factor assumed to underlie the enterprise has largely been ignored by scholars as well as policy makers. We refer here to the role of foreign language (FL) competence in SA.

Part of the problem is that our understanding of this issue has evolved largely within the context of Western European languages and cultures. Because of the accessibility of these languages for native English speakers, it has been possible to take for granted a basic working linguistic competence, for students in regular university courses, in junior-year-abroad programs, and for students going abroad principally to advance their knowledge of the language. Basically, then, FL study as a component of SA has received relatively little attention as a prerequisite to in-country study or as a product of in-country study as compared to other avenues of FL acquisition. There is little research on language study abroad in Western European countries, and practically none has been carried out in non-Western European settings.[2] Of paramount importance to policy makers is the fact that there has been so little formal assessment of the SA experience with regard to language acquisition. Even more to the point, given the fact that SA requires considerable human and financial resources, we still are without any rigorous evaluation of the FL

Reprinted with permission from the *Annals of the American Academy of Political and Social Sciences* 532 (1994):213-225.

component with respect to whether the entire enterprise, as currently conducted, makes the best use of these resources.

In brief, the language issue in SA has evolved in a rather informal, piecemeal fashion, often on the margins of both SA and FL instruction. The resurgence of interest in SA suggests that it is time to begin the formulation of a national planning process aimed at reexamining and redefining the FL role in the SA enterprise and at better integrating and systematizing the various segments of it that have developed in a haphazard manner over time. The purpose of the present article is to frame some of the policy issues that would be integral to such a planning process.

Setting a Policy Planning Context

Any specification of the policy issues in language study and SA must take into consideration the different goals of SA programs, general educational as well as linguistic. Many students go abroad for the general experience of studying in a foreign university, perhaps even for a study program of particular value for their discipline of concentration. Other students, including the majority of students going to non-English-speaking countries, go for the specific purpose of improving FL competence. These two goals, in fact, function together to bind SA and FL study into a close relationship, which can be characterized by the following widely accepted generalization: FL is necessary for SA, just as SA is necessary for FL study.

The success of a SA experience is, to a large extent, dependent upon the student's ability to function in the language of the country of residence. Not infrequently, however, many in-country programs provide special courses in English for visiting Americans (often given by faculty from the students' home institution), as well as enclaved housing and "cultural activities." There is, though, widespread agreement that this kind of reproduction of American education abroad does not adequately replace being able to take advantage of the regular course offerings in a foreign university. Such active participation in the educational system as well as in the culture requires a solid working command of the language of the country.

From the point of view of language acquisition, there is adequate data that indicate clearly that competence in a foreign language requires an extended stay in-country.[3] This is especially true for those languages requiring more time for acquisition by English speakers,[4] although all language fields assume a SA capstone to the language-learning career. In fact, one can distinguish at least three distinct typical tracks for language learning in the United States:

Track A: high school study, plus two years of college instruction, plus junior year SA, plus one year of literature courses in the language;

Track B: perhaps some high school study, plus three to four years of college instruction, plus one to two semesters of language SA, plus continued language study independently or in graduate or professional school; and

Tack C: no high school study, one to two years of college instruction, plus a summer, semester, or year of language study abroad, often in conjunction with other work or study, plus continued independent study.

Track A is typical for French, German, and Spanish students; Track B is characteristic of Arabic, Chinese, Japanese, and Russian. Track C holds for the dozens of other less commonly taught languages (LCTLs) taught in the United States, where course offerings are extremely limited. In each case, however, the goal of functional competence in a FL assumes some period of SA. If these kinds of considerations are valid, then certain obvious policy questions naturally arise concerning FL and SA. With regard to the need for FL competence in SA:

1. To what extent, if any, does success in a SA program depend upon knowledge of a FL?
2. If FL plays a significant role, what level of competence, which skills, and which applications are required for maximum advantage? What kind of language preparation is required, and what kind of language maintenance and enhancement should be provided in-country?
3. If FL competence is not required, then what are the consequences of English only programs in non-English-speaking countries abroad? What is lost under such an arrangement? What kind of accommodations must be made in the in-country environment—in the academic setting and in the living circumstances?

With regard to the efficacy of SA for second language acquisition (SLA):

1. Does SA do something for SLA that domestic instruction cannot? Is the rate of acquisition more rapid? Is there a difference in the acquisition of specific skills in SA as opposed to domestic instruction?
2. What is the cost of the SA effect, particularly as compared with domestic instruction?
3. Does it have this effect for all students? Which students profit most and which least?
4. Are there ways to improve the efficacy of these programs, and what are they?

The intent of the present article is to raise issues with regard to FL and SA, often in the form of questions. Obviously, there is no possibility at this time of providing adequate answers, although some indication of relevant current research will be provided. While keeping distinct the two general goals of SA, we will examine three general themes in this regard: standards and assessment; program design and management; and infrastructure considerations.

Standards and Assessment

It is remarkable that the multimillion-dollar business of SA goes on almost without any reference to standards and assessment. Accreditation is left to the individual institutions and faculty, often leaving in the hands of the program originator and advocate testimony concerning quality and comparability to domestic or other in-country programs. Of course much of the uncertainty concerning general program goals is due to the great diversity of programs and students involved. The range of sending institutions is large, and the goals of their students in studying abroad are many. So, too, the differences in receiving institutions, located in various cultural settings, make the process of standard setting very complex. Noteworthy as well is the more implicit trust in credits earned in Western European programs, where the educational systems most resemble that of the United States, as opposed to the suspicion of credits earned in non-European countries. Indeed, the general issue of accreditation is a major concern today for universities around the world.[5]

Clearly, the general goals of the specific SA program need to be established, and only then can the place of FL be defined. Nevertheless, for SA programs whose goals are broadly educational and not focused exclusively on language acquisition, questions like the following require answers:

1. How much language is required for adequate participation, in order to study in a specific set of university courses as well as to live and interact in the host society?
2. How can these types of skills be measured?
3. How can the general and content-specific linguistic skills be developed prior to the in-country experience, and how can they be supported while the student is living and studying in-country?

For programs that are directed exclusively at FL as a product, other questions demand a response:

1. How much language ability is gained from the in-country experience as contrasted with domestic language study and at what comparable cost?
2. What kinds of skills are enhanced?
3. Is there a real danger that immediate linguistic skills can fossilize in contexts that prize communicative needs over accuracy, that is, can bad habits become so ingrained that they become a permanent part of the language ability of students?
4. Is there a minimum amount of language competence required before a student can interact freely enough to actively acquire more language? If so, what is this threshold?
5. Again, how are these requirements and products to be measured, given the current state of testing and assessment?

Since educational SA programs, by definition, do not target FL enhancement as their principal goal, they assume that participating students have language skills sufficient to the context abroad in which they will be studying. In practice, this sufficiency is produced in two ways: either the student has the FL skills to participate adequately or fully in a foreign university academic program, or the in-country program is modified to accommodate the student's linguistic deficiencies. This modification can take the extreme shape of the American enclave, where students are taught in English by faculty from the home institution, the only difference being that the instruction is carried out on foreign soil. The middle ground is occupied by modifications of these two extremes, often resulting in classes conducted in the host-country language that are truly directed both to developing language and to content knowledge—often with the result being more of the former than the latter.

As noted previously, given the general state of the linguistic competence of American undergraduates, full participation in foreign university programs is generally limited to students who have studied French, German, or Spanish. In these languages, there are students who can actually reach a level of competence adequate to the task of taking courses in-country. The assessment of minimal competence is still problematic, however.[6]

However, if languages like Arabic, Chinese, Japanese, or even Russian are considered, then the situation changes radically. Rare is the student in these languages who is able actually to attend regular university classes in-country. In these languages, as well as in most of the other LCTLs that are taught in the United States, domestic instruction is insufficient to the task of producing students with this capability, either because the languages for native English speakers require much more time to acquire or because only one or two years of instruction are available in domestic programs. Whatever the reason, outside of the principal commonly taught languages in the United States, the standing assumption is that a period of time studying the language in-country is required in order to reach a level of competence that would enable a student to participate freely in that country's university programs. Even for French, German, and Spanish, language study in-country is considered the most effective way to reach this level of competence. Accordingly, the question of standards for and assessment of language programs in-country comes to the fore.

Setting standards and assessment criteria for SA programs specifically designed to enhance FL skills, while certainly problematic, is relatively straightforward, at least on the face of it: the successful SA program designed for FL enhancement is the one that does the most for these skills. Therefore, assessment requires the measurement of these skills before and after the program, the gain being the difference between the earlier measurements and the later ones. The problems involved with this approach are many. The first has to do with the testing instruments themselves, their availability and their design.

Adequate pre- and post-program testing requires standardized proficiency testing instruments, because the in-country experience both presumes and results in general proficiency as opposed to a specified set of domain-specific—for example, medical French, engineering German—skills. The problem is that many languages simply do not have available standardized proficiency tests, let alone for all four language skills (reading, writing, listening, and speaking). This situation means that most programs use surrogates for determining pre- and post-program language proficiency: for example, number of years studying the language, course grades, *ad hoc* teacher recommendations, or special institution- or organization-specific grammar or reading tests. When all students in a dedicated program come from one institution, the use of "seat time," grades, and teacher recommendations often is adequate to the task of determining requisite language knowledge. For programs drawing students from a range of institutions, for obvious reasons, such assessments are less suitable.

While surrogates for proficiency tests may serve as a basis for admitting students to programs, they are less capable of measuring outputs of SA programs and so cannot help in assessing programs based on language gain as determined by subtracting starting skill levels from post-program levels. Clearly, achievement testing, grades, teacher recommendations, and the like are not relevant in a learning environment where a great deal of the learning is assumed to take place outside of the classroom. In this circumstance, only a proficiency test taken by students who have been examined in a proficiency mode before the start of the in-country program will do. Few institutions have the expertise for proficiency testing, and few national SA organizations invest resources in this area, although it would seem to be a necessary part of the selection and assessment process.[7] Even if a full range of proficiency tests and testing expertise existed for a given target country and language, the expense of administering the tests on a consistent basis would be considerable. To make matters even more complex, host-country programs, particularly in the LCTLs, often conduct their own assessment for placement purposes, which may be at odds with the domestically driven assessment approach.

Finally, even for those languages where standardized proficiency tests exist and for those programs that have the resources to administer them, an abiding problem exists in the design of the tests themselves. Tests like the American Council on the Teaching of Foreign Languages Oral Proficiency Interview and the Educational Testing Service's Russian Listening and Reading tests either have only floors and ceilings or are too crude at the more advanced levels to register gains. Thus SA of periods of less than a year often do not produce enough change to be registered on these tests. This is particularly the case for the harder, Class III and IV, languages.[8]

Given these problems with assessing the outputs of SA language programs, another strategy of assessment is called for, one that has the additional capability of providing feedback for program improvement.[9] An ideal language learning interface must be devised for in-country programs, against which any existing model can be compared. This ideal model would be based on the learning that actually takes place in the input-rich immersion environment by being focused on the learning process as such, as opposed to its outcomes. This assessment strategy immediately provides feedback for program improvement as well as student learning improvement. Such a model could then be used as the template for the design of in-country programs. While such a model does not exist, the next section will discuss the components that it will have to contain.

Design and Management of SA Programs

In an ideal universe, the design and management of a teaching environment should be based on the latest SLA research and expertise and focused on the peculiar qualities of that special learning environment as they relate to the learning process. Language study abroad, it could be argued, is the quintessential language-learning environment for adults, given the fact that it approximates most closely the first language-learning circumstance. While a discussion of all the aspects of the learning process as it unfolds in SA is beyond the scope of this article, our discussion here will focus on the primary local conditions under which learning takes place in a SA program: preprogram preparation, in-country learning, and reintegration into the home institution.

Preprogram Preparation

The question of how much FL ability and what particular FL skills are required for a successful SA experience is very complex, as has been indicated. The question of how much language is needed by students in an educational SA program depends on the kind of program that awaits them in-country, in particular on whether there are instructional options in addition to taking regular classes alongside native students. If students are expected to enroll in regular classes, a basic functional level of ability is minimally required. Exactly what this level is can be debated, depending again on the kinds of support structures that can be provided to assist students in this circumstance and on the kinds of residential arrangements that are in place and the language demands they require.

For students whose sole purpose is FL enhancement, there is a broader range of considerations, given the fact that, in principle, there is no assumption that these students can function freely or, for some programs, even minimally in the culture. Assuming that most students can afford to go abroad to study language only once in their educational career, the question of when to send them becomes crucial. How much language ability is needed in order to be able to interact even on a minimal level with natives, assuming that this interaction is the key to acquiring more language and the reason for going abroad in the first place? What is the minimal level of language ability to make this interactivity possible? What is the ideal level? Unfortunately, because of the dearth of research in this area, these questions cannot be answered directly. In fact, there is an inherent problem in addressing the question of the most effective level of language ability for SA, given the learning-curve bias in the standard testing instruments. For example, existing tests will show that four months of Russian will produce a significant jump in ability for novice learners, but most advanced level students will remain at that level.[11] This, of course, does not mean that novices profit most from the experience, but only that the existing tests cannot show the level of language ability needed for a student to profit the most from the SA experience.[12]

Furthermore, the question of student FL preparation involves more than linguistic skills. As Brecht and Walton show, learning a FL includes a number of knowledge bases in addition to the linguistic: meta-learning, cross-cultural communication, and sociolinguistic learning.[13] By "meta-learning" we mean the kind of training that enables the student to become an expert self-manager of the learning of a FL. Given the fact that most language exposure takes place outside of class, beyond the watchful eye of the professional language teacher, it is imperative that students learn how to learn. Particularly in SA, the students are responsible for managing their own learning, including input, intake, and output. Accordingly, adequate preparation for SA would include the development of these self-management skills.

By the same token, the students should be provided with the tools to acquire appropriate cultural behavior and to communicate interculturally. They should also be aware of the sociolinguistic factors that determine successful or failed communication. All of these skills are separate from, although intimately related to, the linguistic skills that normally serve as the content of language courses. It is particularly important for students bound for immersion abroad to achieve a functional ability in all of these skills before departure, although, clearly, all students in all language programs should be given such a learning toolbox.

Research has pointed to other factors that are predictive of student learning abroad, and domestic programs should take them into account. For example, Brecht, Davidson, and Ginsberg report that grammar and reading knowledge is a good indicator of success in the acquisition of speaking skills in-country.[14] While this certainly does not call for a return to the grammar and translation method of FL teaching, it does indicate that a knowledge of grammar is an important tool for a student entering the SA experience.

While the preparation of students for SA should be built into the FL program in the manner previously indicated, the predeparture briefing is an important point of intervention. The problem, however, is that these briefings are often misdirected and ineffective. They are ineffective mostly because they are left as discrete predeparture events with little or no follow-up once the students arrive in-country. These briefings are misdirected, in part because they fail to focus on learning as well as living in the country, the former being as neglected in SA programs as it is in formal FL programs. If self-managed learning has been ignored in the domestic program, attempting to introduce it in an orientation is too little, too late.

In-Country Learning

The design and management of the actual in-country experience, remarkably, remains little informed by research in SLA, mostly because this research is very heavily devoted to the domestic classroom. Whether or not the SA programs involves actual language instruction, there is little doubt that the bulk of the learning opportunities takes place through informal interactions in unstructured environments. The question arises as to how these learning opportunities can be made more effective. How can students manage their own learning in a context that bombards them with linguistic and cultural data, and what can program design do to enhance this process? What is the role of formal, in-country language training in this regard? Answers to these questions require empirical research.[15]

With regard to formal instruction in-country, questions arise as to the role of area or cultural studies in supplementing language training. Both kinds of instruction immediately raise the issue of teacher qualifications, selection, and training. Again, the design of in-country classrooms and curricula must be evaluated, taking into consideration the uniqueness of the SA environment and the expectations of the students. Clearly, it makes no sense to reproduce the American classroom abroad, nor is it logical to expect that native teachers can escape their own teaching traditions, which may or may not be understood by the American student clientele. Again, studies indicate that, for example, a more porous classroom is required for foreign students studying in-country, one that guides more structured language learning and practice outside of the classroom, while still enabling expert monitoring and mentoring on the street. By the same token, the classroom should present opportunities to build upon the learning taking place outside by classroom/mentor debriefing concerning experiences, good and bad, that result from inadequate linguistic and cultural knowledge.

If a program design is intended to take advantage of the SA environment and mitigate its inherent problems, it must be prepared to structure the residential aspects of the student experience. If more learning results from more language use, as is commonly assumed and as Brecht and Wang demonstrate,"[16] then the natural conclusion is that students should live with families in the target culture. However, the management of this mode of housing for large numbers of students causes programs to revert to dormitory living, often with a resident faculty member whose responsibility it is to facilitate the living and learning experience, not necessarily the FL learning experience. In this instance, the issue of enclaving is real, and the question arises as to whether any facilitation of interaction is possible, given the individual personalities and motivations of the students. Perhaps the most important factor here can be the knowledge, based on empirical evidence, that language use is the key ingredient to gain.

Domestic Reintegration

An aspect of SA that has been virtually ignored is how the SA experience can be enhanced upon reentry into the domestic program. Returning students often just do not fit into the advanced language classes, which at best are simulating their in-country experience. While it may be possible to create special sections for these students, more radical adjustments may be called for. For example, these students, particularly the non-language majors, are prime candidates for a language-across-the-curriculum program; and indeed, they may be an important impetus for such an approach. Clearly, the development of self-managed language learning prior to and during SA greatly strengthens the ability of these students to continue in a more self-directed mode upon their return. Also, such students can serve as a resource to the campus and language program, briefing other students interested in SA and serving as peer language tutors.

The Need for a Language Study Abroad Architecture

An effective approach to improving the language component of SA would seem to require at least three kinds of expertise and a means of developing and integrating them, presumably through a new configuration, or architecture. The types of expertise required to design and manage language acquisition in SA include (1) expertise in SLA generally and, in particular, in the application of SLA in the very special context of language study abroad; (2) expertise in the host-country language and culture, including knowledge of its educational traditions; and (3) expertise in the administration and management of language study abroad programs. One serious structural problem with the current approach to language study abroad is that individual institutions typically do not have access to all three expertise bases. Bringing all of them together requires linkage, and bringing them together in an effective, systematic fashion requires planning and policy guidance.

SLA Expertise

The research tradition on how second languages are learned is relatively new, and much of this process is simply unknown. There is, though, a growing literature and expertise base that has to be consulted by program designers and managers. In particular, SLA in SA can be viewed as the mode of second language learning most approximating first language acquisition. Accordingly, research on what happens in-country should be used in the design of domestic language instruction programs, rather than the other way around. In any instance, the expertise base in this regard is still developing and is rarely strong on individual campuses. Therefore, access to this expertise is almost entirely dependent on field, rather than institutional, structures.[17]

Target Language/Culture Expertise

It goes without saying that program designers and managers must have command of the target language and culture, for the success of any prolonged in-country educational experience depends upon how students are prepared for and how the program is adapted to the conditions in-country. This kind of expertise can be found on campuses—in language and area studies programs principally—but also in individual faculty members across the campus. However, often this expertise base does not include an understanding of the educational principles and traditions of the target culture, both in general and as specifically related to language instruction. Again, as a rule, institutions must rely upon the entire language/culture-specific field to provide this expertise, supplementing the local specialists.

Management Expertise

The final type of expertise to be considered is that related to the management and administration, on the domestic side, of language SA programs. This includes such tasks as negotiations with the host-country officials and base institution concerning the program, recruitment of program participants, selection of participants, visa arrangements, insurance and healthcare arrangements, travel abroad, in-country travel, financial management (negotiating the transfer of funds in different currencies), food and housing, the recruitment and selection of resident directors and their salaries, orientation, inspection teams, the awarding and transfer of course credits, the hiring of host country administrators and teachers, program management on a day-to-day basis, and so forth.

This expertise is actually quite well developed at the level of institutions, although few institutions have the personnel and financial resources to expand these services.

Architectural Needs

The issue in any program of language learning whose effective implementation depends upon a level of expertise such as that demanded by SA ultimately rely on a fieldwide architecture.[18] Identifying relevant expertise bases for the language component of SA leads to the even more problematic question of just how these bases are most effectively developed and integrated. As long as SA programs are designed and managed by individual institutions, personnel will determine the outcome of the program.

Access to fieldwide expertise is crucial to the success of almost all institutional exchange and SA efforts. To the extent that such an architecture exists, however, it is a set of SA consortia, generally run by a national or international organization, like the American Council of Teachers of Russian, the American Council for Collaboration in Education and Language Study, and the Council on International Education Exchange, to name the ones with which the authors are best acquainted. The problem is that organizations such as these are in a competitive situation, a condition that does not facilitate cooperation. Nevertheless, all such organizations as well as individual institutions share an interest in improving program quality and cost-effectiveness, both goals seeming to demand some sort of integration and dissemination of expertise in SLA and SA. This integration and dissemination, we contend, is dependent upon an architectural, rather than an institutional, approach. Just what a new architecture for language study abroad would or should look like is, as of now, an open question, and what is presented here are simply rough ideas. The need for such an architecture, however, seems much clearer.

Notes

1. These initiatives include the Senator Edmund Muskie Fellowship Program, the National Security Education Program, the Freedom Exchange and Training Act, and the new initiative within the U.S. Department of Education to begin to work with the European Community on exchanges.
2. A major exception to this assertion is the joint study of language acquisition in SA by the American Council of Teachers of Russian and the National Foreign Language Center. See, for example, Richard D. Brecht, Dan E. Davidson, and Ralph B. Ginsberg, "Predictors of Foreign Language Gain during Study Abroad," *NFLC Occasional Papers* (Washington, DC: National Foreign Language Center, 1993); R.D. Brecht and Jennifer L. Robinson, "Qualitative Analysis Of Second Language Acquisition in Study Abroad: A Case Study of the ACTR/NFLC Project," *NFLC Occasional Papers* (Washington, DC: National Foreign Language Center, 1993).
3. For example, the soon-to-appear study by the National Foreign Language Center of Russian in the United States clearly demonstrates that a basic functional ability in Russian is unlikely to be acquired on the basis of four years of studying Russian in a domestic college.
4. According to Claudia P. Wilds's, "Expected Levels of Absolute Speaking Proficiency in Languages Taught at the Foreign Service Institute" (Internal policy memorandum, Foreign Service Institute, 1973).
5. Recently, the Center for Quality Assurance in International Education was founded under the direction of Marjorie Lenn.
6. For example, the University of California, Santa Barbara's Education Abroad Program has developed a test—the Language Ability Assessment System—to determine a student's ability to take classes in-country.
7. In the United States, to our knowledge, the only organizations that have invested heavily in pre- and post-program proficiency testing have been the American Council of Teachers of Russian and the American Council for Collaboration in Education and Language Study. These organizations, in association with the National Foreign Language Center, have then used these data for research on the process of SLA in SA. See, for example, Brecht, Davidson, and Ginsberg, "Predictors."
8. According to Wilds's, "Expected Levels."
9. Outcome assessments, resulting from proficiency tests like the American Council on the Teaching of Foreign Languages' Oral Proficiency Interview, are incapable of providing feedback regarding program deficien-

cies. They, by design, make no reference to the process by which the outcome skills are obtained and so cannot be used to improve the learning process.
10. See Richard D. Brecht and A. Ronald Walton, "The Case for a Framework for Learner-Managed Foreign Language Learning," *NFLC Occasional Papers* (Washington, DC: National Foreign Language Center, forthcoming).
11. See Brecht, Davidson, and Ginsberg, "Predictors."
12. See Brecht and Robinson, "Qualitative Analysis," for some indication of the kind of data that can be brought to bear indicating that novice students have difficulty learning, while advanced-level students profit most.
13. Brecht and Walton, "Case for a Framework."
14. Brecht, Davidson, and Ginsberg, "Predictors."
15. This kind of research is described in Brecht and Robinson, "Qualitative Analysis."
16. Richard D. Brecht and Xueying Wang, "Evidence of the Role of Language Use in Successful Language Acquisition," *NFLC Occasional Papers* (Washington, DC; National Foreign Language Center, forthcoming).
17. For an outline of such an architecture, see Richard D. Brecht and A. Ronald Walton, "National Strategic Planning in the Less Commonly Taught Languages." *Annals of the American Academy of Political and Social Sciences, 532(1994).*
18. See Brecht and Walton, "National Strategic Planning."

BETWEEN THE IDEA AND THE REALITY

Issues in the Writing and Implementation of the Washington Framework[1]

Chris Brockett

It has been my great privilege and pleasure over the last four years to have had the opportunity to work with a dedicated team of high school teachers and college faculty to develop curricular guidelines for use in Washington State. In September 1994, the project entered a new phase with the publication of a document entitled *A Communicative Framework for Introductory Japanese Language Instruction in Washington State High Schools* through the state Office of Superintendent of Public Instruction. I will not attempt to summarize here the content of this lengthy and complex document that is now beginning to have a significant impact outside our state; a number of outlines have already been published elsewhere. Instead I will speak to some of the philosophical background of the project and the decisions that we made in writing the document. I will then address some challenges that we are now seeing emerge as we move into the implementation stage of the project.

By way of background, I will begin by saying that the project has its origins as a grassroots effort by three dedicated individuals, Leslie Birkland, Masashi Kato, and Mayumi Smith, who sought to coordinate their high school and community college curricula after encountering the widely disparate language skills of students attending an intensive Japanese-language summer camp. With assistance from local organizations, including the Hyogo Culture Center of Seattle, and later the Laurasian Institution and the United States-Japan Foundation (USJF), the project evolved and the committee expanded. Except for a few brief weeks early in the project, the committee did not enjoy any official status or formal affiliation with any organization, and it consisted entirely of volunteers donating their time and energies to a cause that seemed at times to progress at a snail's pace. In the spring and summer of 1994, as the *Washington Framework* finally began to take shape as a document, we were fortunate to receive significant funding from the USJF, and from the Office of Superintendent of Public Instruction in the form of a Chapter 2 grant for innovative projects of statewide significance. These magnanimous grants have allowed us to move beyond writing the document to the far more challenging task of bringing the document to the educational community. Since the fall of 1994, our project has been operating under the auspices of the Japan-America Society of Washington State, which has generously provided its services in managing the grants: this support is testimony to the broad community support for our project.

A Self-Standing Curriculum

Early in our deliberations, the project committee made two key decisions. The first and perhaps, in my view, most central was that the high school Japanese language curriculum should be autonomous, i.e., it should be self-standing, self-motivated, and independent of considerations of what is taught in colleges and universities. This seems somewhat ironic, since one of the original goals of the project was articulation, both across high school programs, and between high schools and higher education. Nonetheless, the idea of legislating directly for articulation was one of the earliest notions that we scrapped as unworkable. A consensus quickly emerged among the committee members that it was not an appropriate objective to seek to prepare students to enter at some arbitrary level, say second year, at a four-year college or university. Although the percentage of Japanese language students advancing to college in Washington State is high, not all go on to college. Moreover, articulation seemed impracticable in light of the spectrum of public and private universities, four year colleges, and community college programs to which Washington State students might advance, with little evidence of coordination among themselves. With a handful of exceptions, college Japanese language curricula, both in Washington State and elsewhere, are woefully underdeveloped and underspecified, their pedagogical objectives and presuppositions unscrutinzed and underevaluated.[2] It is a rare institution of higher education that can point to a coherent, explicit curriculum in Japanese with well-founded objectives from entry through advanced levels. Given present problems of governance of Japanese language programs in higher education, moreover, the colleges and universities seemed to offer small prospect for rational discussion of curricular issues that might spur substantive change within their own institutions, let alone among institutions, or between different levels within the education system.[3]

We concluded that pedagogical objectives of high school Japanese instruction should not be subverted by or subordinated to the sometimes ill-conceived goals of programs in higher education institutions. Instead of trying to ram high school instruction into the Procrustean bed of current college programs, we came to see the role of the project in terms of something other than attempting to mesh high school curricula directly with college programs. First, we decided our document should offer a framework that would enable teachers to provide students with a solid foundation in communicative skills in Japanese, so that they could continue to learn the language successfully for the rest of their lives, independent of whatever college they attended, if they attended college at all. Second, the document would play a central informational role by defining what might be reasonably achievable at the high school level under reasonably good conditions and thereby provide the conceptual foundation for a discourse that would allow university and college faculty to accommodate the students entering their programs with high school language training.[4]

Why Canonize a Mediocrity?

The second, and watershed, decision was a logical consequence of the first. We concluded early on that we should reject the pressures to produce a hastily assembled document that merely codified and canonized an existing mediocrity in the high schools, either by averaging course coverage across a number of programs, or by aggregating the contents of the more commonly used textbooks. We also resisted significant pressures at every step to draw up year-by-year curricular guidelines, since these might tend to be textbook- or methodology-specific. Instead, we tried to delineate a coherent global picture of our objectives—why it is we are attempting to teach Japanese in the high school classroom, and what it is that we are attempting to teach—a picture that could be conveyed to teachers and be utilized by them to guide and inform their day-to-day teaching.

Nor did we wish to justify learning Japanese (or any foreign language, for that matter) in terms of abstract learning goals or putative claims of cognitive development.[5] Eschewing the view that Japanese was to be taught as an abstract exercise, we started with the presupposition that Washington State students are likely to use Japanese, and sought to prepare them to do so. We began by defining the basic goal of Japanese instruction as enabling high school students to communicate in the spoken language for the purposes of short visits to Japan and interactions with Japanese in the United States.

Defining Communication Needs

Having set the focus on language and the communicative use of language, the next step was to consider what communicative skills might be needed for those purposes, and to what extent high school students might reasonably be able to manage those needs at the end of three years. Obviously we could not attempt to define every situation in which high school students might need to use Japanese. However, it is possible to distinguish between the ability to ask someone, say a homestay parent, to take one to a doctor—a valuable, potentially life-saving skill, well within the reach of a high school student—and the more complex task of explaining to the doctor what is wrong, for which the services of a bilingual interpreter may be in order. Similarly, a high school student should be able to get a person to come to the phone, but need not necessarily be expected to sustain the rest of the conversation in Japanese. Having determined a common range of interactional situations in which students might find themselves, we then sought to define curricular content that would allow them to manage those situations linguistically, and might be reasonably achievable in three years in good classroom environments in some not-too-distant future.

For a conceptual and organizational model, our committee borrowed unabashedly from the work of van Ek for the Council of Europe in defining a set of likely topic areas, "communicative skills" (corresponding to van Ek's functions) and "concepts" (corresponding to van Ek's notions).[6] We were not adopting or endorsing the notional/functional approach as a methodology; we have tried very hard to keep the *Washington Framework* methodologically neutral. Nothing in the *Washington Framework* rules out, for example, a structural approach to the introduction of material. The only concern is that instruction never lose sight of the communicative use of language as its objective. The model is particularly useful because it has permitted us to highlight how the grammatical patterns are employed in communication, presenting teachers with a perspective on language that draws them away from the now predominant grammar- and vocabulary-oriented methods that often bear little relation to communication. It allows teachers and students instead to see the immense range of communicative interactions that can be achieved by high school students, even with a relatively small set of grammatical patterns and vocabulary.

Between the Idea and the Reality

We placed the *Washington Framework* document in the hands of the teachers and hoped for communication of the classroom agenda. But the *Washington Framework* is a complex document of nearly 200 pages. It takes close reading in order to begin to absorb it, and at the moment I suspect that its fate is largely to sit on the teacher's bookshelf, or worse, lost in a pile of papers, until it is recycled or the glue on the spine decomposes, whichever comes first. To quote T. S. Eliot perilously out of context, "Between the idea and the reality, between the motion and the act, falls the shadow." The question that we now face is how to bridge the gap that exists between the *Washington Framework* as a document and the reality of the classroom.

It may come as a surprise to many of you to learn that implementation of the *Washington Framework* cannot, under Washington State law, be mandated in the public school system. The Superintendent of Public Instruction in our state is empowered only to notify school boards, principals, and teachers of the existence of the document. Implementation is entirely voluntary, being wholly at the discretion of school districts, schools, and for practical purposes, mostly individual teachers. If the *Washington Framework* is to have any perceptible impact and is to fulfil the desired function of defining a common ground of instruction in the high schools, it must be broadly adopted and utilized by Japanese teachers statewide. The onus thus falls on the project committee to bring the *Framework* to the teachers and explain its contents, their implications, how it can benefit their classrooms, and how to integrate it into their day-to-day teaching. We cannot dictate and we cannot legislate compliance; we can only work to seek its acceptance by members of the Japanese teaching profession, one-by-one, until we achieve a critical mass for a consensus. If we fail to do this, the *Washington Framework* remains destined to languish unread in our own state.

Only now are we beginning to comprehend the appalling dimensions of the task. We have already conducted several weekend workshops on topics concerning the *Framework*, but many more will be needed over the next few years. In July this year, we will be holding a week-long Summer Institute at the University of Puget Sound in order to develop a cadre of teachers who can be well informed about the document and about how they can translate it into classroom practice; we hope to make this institute an annual event. Down the line we will likely need to provide for language training, since although the numbers of non-native teachers in the State with strong Japanese skills is growing rapidly, a significant proportion of teachers will eventually need additional language skills development in order to be able to teach to the *Framework's* communicative orientation.[7] Meetings will be held with principals and administrators to cultivate their interest and support. A series of classroom visits in selected classrooms is being undertaken in the Puget Sound region to see what changes have begun to take place and to assess what must be done to narrow the gap between the *Framework* and reality. Information gained in these visits will be used in planning future workshops and professional skills enhancement programs, designing classroom materials, designing ancillary documents, and preparing a revised edition of the *Washington Framework* document itself.

Towards Ownership and Acceptance

I have come to believe that key to acceptance—and to getting the *Washington Framework* off the bookshelf and open on the teacher's desk—is a sense of ownership and involvement in the process of implementation. Most of the work described above will be undertaken by high school teachers themselves. The *Washington Framework* should be viewed as a conceptual foundation that can *empower Japanese language teachers to manage their own curricula.* It is after all a framework, and it is not intended that teachers go in their classrooms grimly determined to mechanistically carry out its demands. What the document seeks to do is to set forth a coherent vision of the content and goals of high school Japanese language instruction in Washington State. At the risk of being accused of trying to sound like Noam Chomsky, by making a theory precise, we can inquire into and explore the assumptions and consequences of that theory. Now, inquiry into a model can take many forms. It may take the traditional form of academic research in a university setting. Or it may take, as it is now beginning to do, the form of teachers reflecting, individually and collectively, on what they are doing in the classroom in the light of the document, and through that reflection defining, redefining, and refining their curricular objectives and instructional practices.[8]

It is immensely gratifying to see this process of inquiry emerge from within the ranks of Washington teachers. It began with the work of our reaction panel of twelve high school teachers who have participated in the writing of the document. Typical responses to chapter drafts consisted of five-page single-spaced letters—striking evidence, you will agree, of the enthusiasm and commitment that this project has engendered among those involved. A committee of teachers has volunteered to write a sixteen-page study guide to accompany the main document in the hope of making it less intimidating and more approachable. Work will begin during the Summer Institute on drawing up the sample benchmarks, sample lesson plans, and year-by-year curricular guidelines that have long been sought by teachers. With each step we will expand the circle of teachers involved in these activities, and as we do so, the ideas contained in the document will come to be understood more widely and more fully, and will begin, I hope, to constitute the basis of a consensus that will shape Japanese language instruction in Washington State in the next century.

Concluding Remarks: On Increasing Returns

Contrary to the tenets of classical economics, market forces do not guarantee that the best ideas always win. Economists working with the theory of increasing returns have noticed that in industry it is often not the optimal technology that comes to dominate, but the one that was established first that subsequently sets the historical standard. We only need look around us to see how early choices can commit entire societies to designs that turn out in retrospect to be less than ideal. The QWERTY keyboard layout is arguably less efficient and less ergonomically desirable in the modern computer age than many alternative layouts. But computer manufacturers persist with the layout because people have been trained on QWERTY keyboards for generations, and every office has equipment that uses the layout. Similarly, Sony's Beta technology is supposed to have been technologically more advanced than the now-standard VHS system. But more electronics makers used the VHS technology, so more video stores stocked more VHS format tapes because more people owned VHS machines. Before long the Beta technology had vanished from the shelves. Once a society becomes locked into a standard, it becomes massively difficult over time to undo the consequences of the original choice.

We stand at a historical moment when decisions are about to be made that will profoundly affect the shape of high school Japanese language instruction in this country well into the next century. The American Council for the Teaching of Foreign Languages is currently preparing National Standards that will likely have a decisive impact on the directions of instructional policy in the states, and on the policies of the federal and private grant awarding agencies. Oregon, Wisconsin and other states have embarked on well-funded benchmarking projects for Japanese that will have major spillover effects on standards of instruction in other states. It will be vital that these and future efforts do not simply codify the present *status quo*, but that they are informed by knowledge of language and language pedagogy. We are fortunate that high school Japanese instruction is still new enough that it is possible to articulate a clear perspective of what is to be done, and begin to implement those goals without being checked by the inertia of academic tradition. Important choices are about to be made, and we must ensure that those choices are well considered and not hastily arrived at, since the consequences of those choices will be with us for many years to come. Japanese language instruction in the high schools *is* a reality, and a reality that is here to stay. It is going to have to be taken seriously.

Notes

1. This project has been funded by grants from the Laurasian Institution, the USJF, the Japan Foundation, and a Federal Chapter 2 grant administered by the Office of Superintendent of Public Instruction in Washington State. Support has also been provided by the Hyogo Cultural Center, the Japan-America Society of Washington State, and the Jackson School of International Studies at the University of Washington. I would also like to thank these organizations, and especially Tom Foran of the USJF and Judith Billings, Washington Superintendent of Public Instruction, for their long-standing support.
2. With the publication of the National Foreign Language Center's *A Framework for Introductory Japanese Language Curricula in American High Schools and Colleges* and the *Washington Framework*, the curricular guidelines recently developed in Australia, and the efforts currently being made in Oregon, Wisconsin and elsewhere in the country to develop curricular benchmarks, it is fair to say that nationally high schools are considerably more advanced than the colleges in terms of developing an overall conception of what they are trying to achieve in their Japanese language curricula.
3. As higher education funding becomes tighter, language instruction at research-oriented universities tends to be relegated to graduate teaching assistants rather than to trained professionals. This situation may get worse rather than better. This will likely prove a particularly serious problem in departments focused on literary research. The intractability of the governance problem is attested to by the composition of the committee on the TA appointment policy in the Department of Asian Language and Literature at one major research institution with which I am familiar: the four-member committee included specialists in Sanskrit, classical Chinese literature, and 18th-century Japanese literature. That universities should continue to insist that expertise in such fields qualifies individuals to devise policies that will have a profound effect on modern language instruction does not augur at all well for the quality of instruction in modern Asian languages, for internal curricular reform, or for articulation with high schools.
4. It is debatable whether this is politically achievable in traditionalist Asian language and literature departments without vision and forceful intervention on the part of university administrations. Articulation based on high school attainment, such as that currently being attempted on Oregon, where

it is proposed that high school graduates in Japanese will eventually be able to directly enter second-year courses, will entail a significant slow-down in the pace of instruction in many first-year college programs.

5. The ability to communicate with people of another culture in their language is a valuable skill in its own right, requiring no further justification. I am personally inclined to believe that language professionals are often their own worst enemies when they argue that language learning promotes development of cognitive skills, since this devalues the core endeavor of accessing another culture as insufficient justification in its own right. Such arguments are reminiscent of the old-time classicists' regarding assertions that learning Latin teaches students discipline. It did not work for classicists, and it will not work for modern language teachers either. We teach foreign languages in our schools because we value, and wish our children to have access to, the things that the societies that speak those languages have to offer us.

6. We modified van Ek's original terminology when it was found to be too opaque for many teachers. We did not wish the message of the document to be obscured or ignored because of unfamiliar terminology.

7. The *Washington Framework* suggests that teachers have at least 600 hours of communication-oriented language training, or 450 hours plus at least six months experience in Japan. Interestingly, this aspect of the document was strongly endorsed by the teachers at reaction and panel meetings. I believe this reflects the desire for professional recognition, and an acknowledgment that Japanese teaching in the schools will continue to be peripheralized by school administrators until more rigorous professional standards are in place. It is of little help to teachers that Washington State persists in requiring only one year of coursework and a pass in the New York State University examination in order to obtain a teaching endorsement for Japanese.

8. One area of professional development that may be necessary is training in descriptive and applied linguistics. Many teachers report themselves quite daunted by even the limited quantity of linguistic terminology encountered in our document. If one of our themes must be professional empowerment, a knowledge of the basic principles of grammatical analysis, pragmatic strategies, sociolinguistics and discourse must be part of a language teacher's professional conceptual tool kit.

SHAPING THE NEXT GENERATION

A Look at Teacher Training

Eleanor H. Jorden

As the enrollment figures for Japanese language classes bring this language to the fourth or fifth[1] most commonly taught in the United States, and programs extend further and further downward, all the way to the kindergarten level, the shortage of professionally trained teachers grows ever more acute. At every conference on the needs of the field, it would seem, the conclusion is that the training of more language teachers must be our number one priority.

This is not an unreasonable decision. It is the teacher, after all, who ultimately determines the quality of classroom instruction. The best of language teaching materials can be ruined by a poor teacher and, in contrast, inferior materials can be compensated for, to some extent at least, by a well-trained, professional instructor. And for the student working with the most advanced multimedia software, there comes a time when interaction with a skilled teacher becomes necessary.

New teacher training offerings have been springing up everywhere as a result of the emphasis on the need, but many are organized and taught by instructors who have never themselves undergone any training—even as language teachers, much less as trainers of teachers. And there are still those who assume that native speakers are, of course, by virtue of being native speakers, able not only to teach but also to train teachers of their language. These training opportunities vary from one- and two-day workshops to nine week intensive summer programs and academic-year-long courses. Recently, graduate degree programs specifically on Japanese language pedagogy are beginning to crop up in universities around the country.

When we talk about the training of teachers of Japanese in the next century, we need to examine the current offerings very carefully. Are we really *training* teachers? Are we offering serious guidance on how to practice a particular profession so as to achieve stated goals, or are we merely describing isolated classroom techniques and introducing a cross section of approaches to language teaching, with particular emphasis on the latest fad?

Sophisticated training for teachers of Japanese is particularly necessary because of the nature of this "truly foreign language." For the American student, Japanese is one of the most difficult foreign languages in which to gain meaningful competency. It presents a double challenge: First is the linguistic code, totally different from that of English. Many linguistic features the English speaker has come to expect to find in all languages (for example, the distinction between singular and plural and the agreement between subject and verb) are missing, but new, unfamiliar patterns are to be found in virtually every utterance. Second is the cultural code, reflecting the behavioral culture of Japanese society, the influence of which permeates the language. Again we find a system that presents tremendous contrast with its American counterpart. The American who tries to arrive at Japanese simply by translating the English language that would be appropriate in a given situation has little chance of producing authentic Japanese. How to handle these two codes, both of which are difficult for the American learner, is pedagogically difficult for the Japanese language teacher.

Some of our so-called training offerings are introducing students to countless methods, from suggestopedia to total physical response, from the silent way to the communicative approach, without any clear indication as to their relative validity. How are new trainees to know how to proceed? What is their basis for judgment? Missing is any serious discussion of the basic, underlying assumptions that relate to language and the effect they should have on arriving at a unified approach to language pedagogy that demonstrably achieves superior results.

What is totally missing from so much of our training is the concept of the unified *program*. In institution after institution we find Japanese offered as a series of independent courses, each taught by a teacher who is not just permitted, but actually encouraged, to follow his/her own prejudices. The poor student is not unlike a hospital patient being treated by a medical staff, not one of whom agrees with any other on what constitutes appropriate treatment. When the situation becomes really serious, one staff member will actually tell the patient how incompetent his/her colleagues are.

Contrary to the lack of professional attention it usually receives, language teaching is actually an extremely complex field, much more so than most realize. Unlike pedagogy that requires only the transfer (and sometimes, interpretation) of information—for example, "Washington was the first president of the U.S."—language teaching has both a cognitive component ("fact") and a skill component ("act"). It takes only a comparatively short time to explain the difference between a -*masu*-form and a -*masita*-form ("fact" information), but it takes an enormous amount of "act" practice before students consistently give up uttering sequences like *kinoo ikimasu* "yesterday I go/will go." Acquiring knowledge and acquiring a skill become very different challenges for the language student, as do having *and* transferring both these components for the teacher.

When we move to the skill area of our society, we think immediately of sports and their coaches. Or we can continue our medical analogy. Imagine training a surgeon by saying: Every student for him/herself; you've been taught the relevant knowledge; now use that scalpel according to whatever method you choose. Imagine granting drivers' licenses to applicants who have never had any on-the-road training. If we are to develop adequate training programs for language teachers, they must include coverage of the skill component. And keeping in mind the concept of 'program,' we must train participants who will become good team players, working cooperatively with their leader—the coach or program coordinator or department chair or whatever the designation—who is ultimately responsible for the direction of the program and its success (or lack thereof).

Of course, good teacher trainers should include in their curricula discussion of all methodologies that are current and explain in detail the reasons for the choice of one over the others. The ultimate justification must, of course, be the product, i.e. the language competence of the graduates. Any member of a team should certainly be encouraged to make suggestions for changes, provided they can be justified. If they prove to be worth adopting by one, then they should be adopted by all. Doesn't it make sense for *all* members of the team to use what appears to be the most generally effective methodology?

A meaningful, substantive teacher training program should have at least three components: (1) a lecture component, (2) an observation component, and (3) a trainee demonstration component. The lecture component should cover the spectrum of knowledge the trainee requires, including such topics as the goals of the course—the general assumptions of language pedagogy, the basic philosophy of the program, and the methodology being used *and why*—guidance on how to teach each of the four skills, analysis of good teaching materials, evaluation of student performance, effective testing techniques, and language learning outside of the formal language program. During the observation component, the trainees observe master teachers instructing actual classes, using the principles explained during the lecture component. And during the trainee demonstration component, all course participants would teach actual class sessions that would later be individually critiqued by a faculty member. It is not difficult to see why each of these course components is absolutely essential. After observing sessions that demonstrate the recommended methodology, which has been thoroughly explained and justified during lectures, trainees must then be able to prove their own ability to perform successfully in the classroom. The teacher who can describe teaching but can't teach is as useless as the language student who can talk about a language but can't speak it.

The ideal instructor is one who is talented, trained, and experienced. Without some degree of inborn talent, it is unlikely that all the training and enthusiasm in the world will produce a superior teacher. On the other hand, talent alone will never free one from the need for professional training. Those with talent quickly rise to the head of the class in a teacher training program, but I have never encountered a so-called 'born teacher' of Japanese who wasn't in serious need of the entire content of a training program curriculum.

An error that is frequently made is to believe that experience alone can substitute for training. Countless Japanese language teachers are hired every year on the basis of their experience. But what kind of experience? In the words of Hector Hammerly: "Practice does *not* necessarily make perfect, but it does make permanent." A bad teacher, with experience, can become truly good at being bad! There is no question that experience, following training, enables a language instructor to gain confidence and to incorporate the principles of his or her training with increased assurance. Experience is, of course, extremely important in the development of a highly skilled teacher, but that experience must be grounded in accurate pedagogical principles. Consider, now, the well-qualified applicant for a Japanese teaching position—

a talented, highly motivated individual with the academic degrees required for the position, who has completed an excellent training program, maintaining an outstanding record, and has had several years of teaching experience with superior recommendations. Given the critical need for Japanese language teachers, could there possibly be anything that would prevent someone with these credentials from being an immediate and continuing success in the field of Japanese language teaching?

Unfortunately there is a potential enemy: governance. As examples, let me list nine tragic scenarios that frequently occur.

1. A well-trained instructor, at the lecturer level, has established and developed an excellent Japanese language program at a small college. It has been enthusiastically received by the students and is flourishing. The college decides that the program is so successful that it is ready to take on a tenure-track junior professor. A Ph.D. in Japanese literature with absolutely no training, experience, or interest in elementary-level language teaching is hired and the successful lecturer is fired.
2. A well-trained and experienced pedagogical linguist (a junior professor) in a large university with a very large Japanese language program is hired to run the program. The task is tremendous, involving not only reorganization, lecturing, curriculum development, scheduling, staffing, counseling, etc., but also the training of untrained staff who were on board before his arrival. He is doing an excellent job, but is let go after his initial contracts are up because he hasn't published sufficiently.
3. A well-trained and experienced specialist in Japanese language pedagogy, who holds a Ph.D. in linguistics, is hired at a junior level and placed in charge of the Japanese language program. She has constant opposition and interference from a senior professor in an unrelated discipline involving Japan, who has absolutely no background in language teaching. The senior professor is influential in having the linguist denied tenure and terminated.
4. The chair of a department that includes both language and literature courses is herself a literature specialist. When an opening in the department occurs, the chair sees an opportunity to round out the literature program with a specialist in the pre-modern period, in spite of a critical need for another language specialist to help handle the overflow of language students. There

is very little demand for the additional literature specialist. The chair, with senior colleagues, prevail.

5. One of the responsibilities of university professors is to locate funding for their graduate students. When those students are in the field of Japanese literature or linguistics, the obvious solution is assistantships in the Japanese language program. In some cases, even graduate students in totally unrelated fields may also be given assistantships in the Japanese language program, if they happen to know Japanese. In most universities, very little—if any—training is provided for these assistants: an all too common procedure is to hand them a copy of the textbook and the schedule and wish them luck. To make matters worse, many of these graduate students have little or no interest in language teaching—to say nothing of their lack of competence. Openings for appropriately trained instructors are lost.

6. Junior professors of Japanese linguistics and literature are hired in departments which have no course openings in their areas of expertise. With assurance that someday they will work their way up to teaching classes in their specializations, they are assigned to assistantships as language teachers, in spite of a lack of training or interest. Again the appropriately trained specialist is not hired.

7. New instructors, well-trained in modern Japanese language pedagogy, join an experienced but totally untrained faculty. The inferior results achieved by the students make clear that the program has a serious problem, but the new members are unable to bring about needed change when rank, seniority, rigidity and, in some cases, gender all operate against them. They immediately look for a new position.

8. A high school instructor has enrolled in an intensive training program that lasts for an entire summer. Returning to school in the fall, fired up with a desire to put to use everything she has learned and to introduce a new textbook, she is informed that the textbook already in use cannot be changed for the next 5 years. She considers looking for another position.

9. In many (most?) high schools, the hiring of faculty is the responsibility of the principals, even though they rarely know anything about the Japanese language or its teaching. For many, the locating of a native speaker, with or without teacher training experience, solves their problem. This reflects the persisting myth that all native speakers are qualified to teach their

native language, simply because they know the foreign language in question. Well trained applicants are not sought out.

If the next century is to be a landmark period for the reorganization of Japanese language teaching in the U.S., we need bold measures in the restructuring of our faculties. Language teaching must be recognized as very different in nature from the teaching of theoretical linguistics or literature or history. The linguistic analysis of the language—involving phonology, morphology, syntax, discourse analysis, sociolinguistics, and pragmatics—is a matter of linguistic knowledge, but the practical application of this knowledge moves the instruction over to the skill area and, as we mentioned before, the transfer of a skill is different from the transfer of facts. Students whose training and competence is limited to talking *about* the language in their own language, to translating isolated sentences into Japanese, to filling in the blanks in grammatical exercises, and such, will never be able to use Japanese communicatively in an authentic style. And after all, communication is the primary purpose of language. This complicated, double-barreled nature of language teaching should hardly relegate it to the second-class status it often holds.

Not everyone in the field can be expected to handle the entire range of requirements of a language program. We need to recognize a hierarchy of ranks, each representing a different type of job. From an entry level technician to a tenured professor, the responsibilities range from drill class instruction to lecturing on linguistic analysis, training new instructors, pedagogical research, etc. All requiring training their particular responsibilities but their responsibilities will be different. A fact that must never be forgotten is that the special skills of native and non-native teachers are complementary, not identical. To the extent that a program can have both types of teachers, its curriculum can be enhanced.

"Publish or perish" should not be strictly applied to pedagogical specialist. In addition to publishing on pedagogical subjects, they should be given credit for involvement in significant activities related to pedagogy: Are they the authors of published teaching materials, used in programs beside their own? Do they train language teachers in their own and other programs? Do they serve as instructors in special teacher training programs? Do they serve as consultants for pedagogical projects, including test development? Do they conduct pedagogical research?

High school certification as a teacher of Japanese is now available in a number of states, but the basis for certification must be reexamined. Above all, it should not be simply a language competency examination, which in no way identifies a skilled, well-trained language teacher. It has been encouraging to note that recent applicants for college Japanese teaching positions are more and more frequently required to teach an actual class as part of their application process. At least a taped demonstration should definitely be part of any certification procedure, for any level of instruction.

It is important to consider what role technology should play in the Japanese language programs of the future. With carefully designed, pedagogically sophisticated teaching materials, transferred appropriately to multimedia formats, extremely useful programs can be developed that are capable of taking over the more routine tasks of the classroom. Such programs are at the present time being created for Japanese. But they can never be better than the material and pedagogy that underlie them, and on that point they must be carefully examined. Undoubtedly the ideal multimedia programs will be more successful than the unskilled classroom teacher who has little idea of how to teach a language. However, they can never replace the highly skilled instructor who alone, supplementing the type of material that a machine can handle with excellent results, can provide the capacity for unpredictability that is the hallmark of natural language. Can a machine ever predict, "Excuse me, Mr. Blank, but I think your wastepaper basket is on fire," as a possible reply to the question "What do you think of the current political crisis in Nashirazu?"

But what can be done to alleviate the governance problems? As a start, short two- to three-day intensive workshops for administrators and department chairs might be offered, during which lectures on the challenges involved in teaching a 'truly foreign language' are supplemented by exercises in problem solving, using examples like those mentioned above. Such workshops, if offered during a teacher training workshop, would enable these administrators to observe the kind of training that teachers of Japanese require, thereby helping them to make administrative decisions leading to improved programs.

The field of Japanese language pedagogy is still young, but old enough to have developed a few truly outstanding practitioners. How valuable it would be if the old practice of apprenticeship were revived and formalized; if it were possible for those beginning their careers to follow their introductory training with a period of apprenticeship to a master mentor, observing his/her classes and being observed during their own instructional sessions for at least an academic year. Academic credit should be granted for such training, following a final exam not unlike that given to musicians: a demonstration, before a group of qualified examiners, of ability to *practice* the profession.

The proof of good pedagogy lies, of course, in the product that is produced. Next after teacher training, we need to work seriously on the development of truly sophisticated measurement instruments to evaluate the performance of program graduates. Acknowledging the differences in language learning aptitude, motivation, and application one expects to encounter among learners in any program, with sufficient numbers it will undoubtedly become obvious that trained teachers do indeed make a difference in outcomes.

Learners do not remain in formal programs indefinitely. Included within that portion of training should be instruction on how to proceed independently later. Language learning is, after all, a lifetime learning activity. But one thing is clear: advanced proficiency cannot be built on a weak, inaccurate base without disastrous results. Thus the influence of teachers handling the beginning and intermediate levels of language instruction extends far beyond what occurs in their classes. We must never forget "First in, last out": the first things learned are the last to be forgotten—and this applies equally to mistakes and bad linguistic habits as well as accurate control of a language.

The range in quality found in the Japanese language programs of today is vast—from our cutting edge programs, which are certainly among the very best in the world, to those that are undoubtedly among the worst. We must demonstrate throughout the field what can actually be accomplished by Japanese language learners when they enjoy the instruction of a truly superior, well trained teacher. As long as so many instructors, having no idea of how much better things could be, are content with what turns out to be more than mediocrity, there will be little movement forward. Our hope for significant progress will depend on the proliferation of the significant gains in pedagogy made by the leaders in the field.

Note

1. After Spanish, French, and German, and tied with Italian.

CURRICULUM DESIGN

Teaching Japanese in the Humanities

Emiko Konomi

Recently one of my colleagues told me an interesting story about an experience she had during a visit to Australia. Japanese is the most commonly taught foreign language in Australian schools; according to the Japan Foundation, the number of students studying Japanese has increased one thousand percent in the last ten years in that country. During her visit, my colleague met a Japanese language teacher who said that Japanese was taught just like any other foreign language in his school because "Japanese is just another foreign language." Not knowing what the teacher meant, my colleague asked how he taught all the many varieties of style and different politeness levels, the linguistic features perhaps most characteristic of Japanese. The teacher responded, "Oh, those? We ignore them."

As much as my colleague was appalled by this response, her Australian friend's attitude seems more often the rule than the exception even in the United States. Nevertheless, Japanese is a language with no socially neutral expressions. For example, even to say "thank you" properly in the range of situations one encounters in everyday life requires that the learner understand the different grammatical forms for indicating gratitude that depend on the social status of the speaker and the addressee and on their familiarity with one another. It is, therefore, obvious that a large amount of attention must be devoted to understanding cultural contexts from the first moment of instruction, if the learner is to communicate effectively. Some Japanese pedagogists hold that this component of Japanese teaching and learning is the most important and the most challenging. Nevertheless, this issue is ignored in many Japanese language programs, particularly when the curriculum is designed in accordance with existing models of teaching languages that share little structurally and culturally with Japanese.

It is common knowledge that Japanese is one of the toughest languages for native speakers of English to master. The Foreign Service Institute of the Department of State and the Defense Language Institute have both divided the various languages they teach into four categories based on the number of hours of study it takes on average for native English speakers to attain a prescribed level of proficiency. Category I languages, the easiest, include French, German, and Spanish. Japanese is placed in Category IV, the most difficult, along with Arabic, Chinese and Korean. Proficiency is rated on a scale from zero (no functional proficiency) to five (the proficiency of an educated native speaker). According to the FSI, a student with average language learning aptitude requires 480 contact hours to reach proficiency level 2 in a Category I language, but 1,320 contact hours to reach the same proficiency in a Category IV language. These data show why a more intensive approach to instruction in Japanese is required, particularly at the beginning of the curriculum, than in Western European languages.

What makes learning Japanese so time-consuming for native English speakers? The difficulty of the writing system is often given a disproportionate attention by teachers of Japanese, particularly those who are Japanese themselves. This is probably because the writing system was the biggest if not only challenge they consciously had to work on in their own education. For non-Japanese students, however, challenges come not only from the exotic writing system but also from components of the language that must be mastered before training in reading and writing can even begin: our students have to master unfamiliar phonological distinctions, including pitch accent, a rich and complex inflectional system, grammatical patterns and semantic categories unknown in English, and the patterns of discourse structure favored by Japanese speakers.

Though often overshadowed by the writing system, these differences between the linguistic codes of Japanese and English are at least fairly well known. Both they and the writing system tend to overshadow how the Japanese language is used within various social contexts in Japan and how communicative intentions are encoded as language. This area includes the pragmatics of interpersonal and interpretive communications that have close relation to the culture. It is the area where language usage interfaces with the mindset and behavioral patterns of Japanese society in general. Learners discover that they cannot simply transfer explicit statements, questions, requests, or other kinds of utterances from English into Japanese; they must instead see the world from a Japanese viewpoint and learn to encode their intentions, given this new perception, into Japanese utterances. For example, Japanese tend to avoid giving direct orders and bluntly saying "no" to a request; they tend to be vague or ambiguous when discussing sensitive matters; they readily speak in a self-effacing manner; they pay great attention to in-group/out-group affiliations. Americans relying only on their "instincts" and intuitions may see these sociolinguistic behaviors as defensive, manipulative, or even disingenuous, and have a hard time bringing themselves to accept and use them when speaking Japanese. They need to receive explicit instruction and training in overcoming this cultural gap just as much in handling the linguistic code correctly.

The problem is aggravated by the fact that there is relatively little understanding of these issues among Japanese language educators. Anthropologists such as Edward T. Hall (1951) and, most recently, Michael Agar (1994) have called attention to the inseparability of language from its cultural setting, and there is, of course, a research literature on Japanese sociolinguistics and discourse analysis. However, few scholars have applied these results in a systematic way to the development of Japanese language curricula.

A major part of the problem seems to be a confusion about the term culture itself. Hammerly (1982) divides the teaching of culture in the context of foreign language instruction into three categories. The first is Achievement Culture, such as the fine arts, literature, music, crafts, and other aesthetically evaluated activities. In the case of Japan, traditional arts such as flower arrangement, the tea ceremony, and the various kind of theater, music, and martial arts fall into this category. The second is Informational Culture, which includes the geography of the country, its political system, history, and so forth. The third area is Behavioral Culture, which includes all those beliefs and attitudes that make up the mindset of the society and underlies its behavioral patterns. The first two types of culture are deliberately studied and learned by natives in school, in special lessons, or through reading, but the Behavioral Culture is acquired without awareness or conscious effort. Jorden (1991) points out how this important difference between Achievement and Informational Culture, on the one hand, and Behavioral Culture, on the other, parallels the difference between acquired language (L1) and learned language (L2). Acquired culture, like one's native language, is gained without awareness and becomes so much a part of natural, automatic, daily behavior that one tends to see it as a universal norm of human behavior; nevertheless, the foreign student must consciously learn it, just as he or she must consciously learn the language.

In intercultural communication, differences in Achievement and Informational Cultures may be small or irrelevant, but differences in Behavioral Culture can be enormous and, in any case, are always a potential source of misunderstanding. Not knowing where Mt. Fuji is located, or not knowing how to make *origami*, for example, will never be as damaging as not knowing how to express disagreement with discretion or how to turn down an invitation politely. Among European languages, where the gaps in Behavioral Culture are relatively small, equal or greater emphasis seems to be placed on the teaching of Achievement Culture and Informational Culture than on Behavioral Culture in the foreign language classroom. Indeed, students are often taught the Achievement and Informational Culture of a given European society through the target language itself; this is possible because of the simplicity of the writing systems involved and the high degree of overlap in Behavioral Culture, both of which allow for relatively early reading of authentic materials. This in turn tends to put a focus on literature and an anecdotal approach to Behavioral Culture. Rarely, for instance, does a student of French get a chance to talk about French society with a specialist in French political science or sociology. The close association of literature with the study of the language code is one of the most noticeable characteristics of instruction in Western European languages.

On the other hand, in Japanese, the complexity of the language itself is so great that there is simply no time to attempt a systematic introduction to thousands of years of Achievement and Informational Culture in a language course. Keep in mind that, in many institutions, it is assumed that all foreign languages can and should be taught using the same schedule of credits and contact hours. If time for Japanese language instruction is spent on Achievement and Informational Culture, the remaining time for Behavioral Culture and language will be significantly reduced. It is therefore imperative that Achievement and Informational Culture be taught in separate courses by area studies experts and that the teaching of Behavioral Culture be well integrated into the language curriculum. Moreover, since mastery of the language—especially the written language—takes a long time to develop in a Category IV language, it is not realistic to teach Japanese civilization through the Japanese language at elementary levels of instruction; such work can be handled far more efficiently in English.

It is unfortunate that the cultural component of many Japanese classes turns out to be nothing but an introduction to the Achievement and Information Cultures of Japan. Video and laser discs, along with various new technologies, are widely used these days, but in many cases they are simply electronic versions of printed guidebooks to temples, scenic locations, works of art, and the like. Video used in this manner does little to teach foreigners how to interact effectively with native speakers, whatever it may do for their general education. For effective language instruction, video should be used to give students a chance to observe conversations in which native speakers behave in a socially and linguistically normal way. A video can show facial expressions, gestures, and eye contact as well as a record of the speech used. All these elements play a part in the process of communication and all send out important messages. Videos that show total conversational situations in a way that allows a skilled teacher to use them as part of an integrated curriculum can therefore be of great value; on the other hand, random clips from Japanese television or pictures of Japanese at work and play with voice-overs in Japanese beyond the students' current levels of understanding serve no purpose in terms of the goals of basic language instruction.

Just as not all videos are appropriate for use in language classrooms, so too, care must be exercised in recommending the use of interactive self-teaching computer programs. Though wildly popular these days, I know of none so far in which the audio component has been adequately integrated into the package. Even though better programs will probably be developed along the lines of the better-quality videos available today, the technology for continuous speech analysis by different speakers is still costly and unreliable; these limitations will be with us for a long time to come. In the meantime, it is obvious that students have to provide written input. This is done only if one requires active production of romanized script or else rushes into written Japanese. Both these alternatives entail changing pedagogical priorities simply for the sake of using technology, using a non-authentic form of Japanese writing, or both, and so are not acceptable. As Unger, Granich, and Hatasa (1992) point out, no application of technology can accelerate mental process directly. As with all skill learning, daily practice using the skill in real-life situations is indispensable. Even if one could program a computer simulation of the acting out of a dialogue in a classroom, there would be no way to compel a student to actively use language while running the program or to check the quality of the speech he/she produced. Computers are no miracle machines. Successful use of computers relies on the quality of the entire curriculum.

This brings me to the issue of teaching Japanese in relation to the humanities. In American and European education, modern languages were not even a recognized discipline until the end of the last century. It was simply assumed that one would learn modern languages, primarily for the purposes of reading, as part of one's education. Only the classical languages had traditional academic standing. When the modern languages of Europe finally gained respectability, they were viewed as additions to the traditional humanities. As "exotic" languages like Chinese and Japanese made their appearance, they were expected to fit the same mold; this is how they were taught in departments of "Oriental Languages" in America up to World War II and how they are still taught in many places in Europe. The practical needs of the war gave rise in the United States to a more proficiency-oriented approach to Japanese language teaching, but this development had limited influence. Most university departments changed their names from "Oriental" or "Far Eastern" to "East Asian" during the Cold War when the federal government pumped money into area studies programs, but language teaching continued largely as before, though on a somewhat larger scale. Even today, despite the vogue for "proficiency-oriented" curricula and "communicative competence" in the classroom, even a casual review of the textbooks and methods being employed at most schools shows that the primary goal is to get students into reading as quickly as possible. A sound internalization of the linguistic code, let alone of the Behavioral Culture involved, is still a lower priority.

I see no particular reason to continue to give literary studies a privileged position in the field of Japanese language teaching. This situation is the understandable result of historical circumstances, but it fails to take the special characteristics of Japanese as a Category IV language into account. After two or three years of a Western European language, it may not be unreasonable to given students a bilingual dictionary and expect them to read literature in the original. In the case of Japanese, two years of college study is merely an introduction to the language, and thus it is highly questionable whether students can benefit from such a practice, leaving major goals behind in the overall linguistic training. It seems to me that it would make much more sense to treat Japanese for the study of literature as a case of "language for special purposes" to be reserved for the graduate-level and very strong undergraduate programs.

The contribution that Japanese language courses can make to the humanities and liberal education in general is not primarily in teaching a few highly talented students how to read Japanese literature in the original, but rather in teaching the overwhelming majority of students about the close interrelationship between language and culture. A well-taught language course should not only train students to get along linguistically in Japan but should also heighten their awareness of both their own culture and that of Japan. Even if they never pursue the study of Japanese to the point where they can read Japanese novels with ease, students should be able to approach literature and other humanities with an awareness of what lurks beneath the surface of the translations in terms of cultural differences. Surely, such discernment is the key humanistic value that informs liberal education.

The most radical change that has characterized Japanese language instruction in the 1980s is its entry into the educational mainstream. According to MLA statistics (Brod 1988), the highest rate of enrollment growth in the United States at the college level is in Japanese, with a 45 percent enrollment growth between 1983 and 1986. That was a decade ago. Now Japanese is the fourth most commonly taught foreign language in the country, ranked only after Spanish, French, and German. It is no longer surprising to hear that some children are learning Japanese in so-called immersion classes in kindergarten. Foreign language educators have long tried to create a rationale for the centrality of foreign language study in the American educational system. Yet the mainstreaming of Japanese has been generated by external forces such as anxiety over economic competitiveness. Historically, Japanese programs enjoyed the luxury of working with small numbers of highly motivated and often linguistically gifted students. The typical Japanese students came with curiosity and a plan, however vague, to use the language in some way as part of a postgraduate career. This picture has changed radically in the last decade. The urgent problems facing Japanese language programs today have to do with their newly gained mainstream status. These include demands to offer

Japanese courses where none were offered before, to expand existing programs to cater to higher enrollments and more heterogeneous student bodies, to reexamine the curriculum to meet "special needs," and to have national and state-level curriculum guidelines and standardized assessment devices. The initial approach to answering these demands has often been to follow the lead of Western European languages or, in some cases, the ESL model. Such attempts often fail because they typically neglect the crucial differences between Japanese and those languages.

Given the frustrations with these failed approaches, it is not at all surprising that some Japanese educators have stressed the value of the study experience itself or the value of "giving a taste of Japan" to a wider range of students, in effect giving up on the direct goal of developing functional language skills. Nor is it rare that an introductory Japanese course, although designed to teach the language, ends up being more like a course on Japanese civilization; in many cases, the course ends up talking *about* the language while students rarely talk *in* the language. Responses of this kind are, I think, unacceptable. When faced with the need for change, hard choices must be made between whether to continue the traditional curriculum or change the paradigm. Ideally, a program can offer two tracks: one reserved for the intensive area-studies needed by those who plan to use Japanese for a postgraduate career, and the other open to a wider range of students. This kind of two-track arrangement is certainly not unusual in the sciences, and it seems to be a reasonable option to be explored in some programs with large enrollment; of course, the particular circumstances of each program and institution must be taken into account.

Perhaps the making of choices will be facilitated by recent nationwide efforts in the field of Japanese language toward standardization through curriculum and assessment systems. A national standardized proficiency test has been developed; curriculum guidelines for colleges and high schools have been published, and several similar documents at the state level have been announced. Although their impact on the field of Japanese education is yet to be assessed, there is no doubt that they will build a consensus on a national standard for Japanese language instruction in the United States. To the extent that standard will inevitably be different from that of Western European languages or for ESL, this turn of events should have positive consequences.

There is a challenge here and one that involves the integrity of the field of Japanese education itself. The challenge is to become proactive rather than reactive in expanding the field of Japanese language education in its newly gained mainstream status. What is involved in the process is not to simply follow the existing models of other foreign languages, but rather to establish a vision of our own.

References

Agar, Michael. (1988) "Foreign Language Enrollments in U.S. Institutions of Higher Education Fall 1986." Association of Departments of Forcign Language Bulletin 19: 39-44.

Hall, Edward T. (1959) *The Silent Language.* Greenwich, Connecticut: Fawcett Publication.

Hammerly, Hector. (1982) *Synthesis in Second Language Teaching: An Introduction to Linguistics.* Blaine, WA, Second Language Publications.

Jorden, Eleanor H. (1991) "The Use of Interactive Video in the Learning of Japanese." In *Foreign Language Acquisition Research and the Classroom*, Ed. B. Freed, 384-392. Lexington, Massachusetts, DC Heath.

Unger, J. Marshall, Ron Granich, and Kazumi Hatasa. (1992) *McTAVISH: Final Report of the Mini-Committee on Telecommunications, Audio-Visual Materials, and Instructional Software and Hardware*, Association of Teachers of Japanese.

WHO OWNS THE JAPANESE LANGUAGE CURRICULUM?

Shigeru Miyagawa

Almost fifteen years ago, I was put in charge of designing the Japanese language program at the Ohio State University. In collaboration with colleagues, particularly Galal Walker, my counterpart in Chinese, we embarked on designing a language curriculum that focused on oral skills. We wanted to make sure that our students could at least speak and listen to Japanese well. This meant that we had to reduce the number of *kanji*, and I even instituted the use of romanization, which, frankly, I detested at the time and, to this day, I can't read very well. Of course, I wasn't the one learning Japanese, and, observing my students as they made the transition to the new curriculum, I was pleased at how relatively quickly they attained spoken and listening skills. That was the happy part of the story. Very soon after we began to install this curriculum, I began to receive complaints. Not from the students. But from my own colleagues in humanities and social sciences. I still recall vividly the conversation. They argued that I was doing a terrible disservice to their advanced undergraduate students and graduate students, by handicapping them in reading. They were outraged by the new curriculum. The question that popped into my head was, "who owns the Japanese language curriculum?" To finish this part of the story, we went ahead and implemented a language curriculum that privileged oral skills. I did this in the belief that those of us in the East Asian Languages and Literatures department were the sole owners of the language curriculum.[1]

Recently, I have been asking myself the same question that popped into my head fifteen years ago, "who owns the Japanese language curriculum?" I

This article is also published at the following web site: http://www-japan.mit.edu/articles/curriculum.html

am no longer certain that the Japanese teaching professionals will continue to possess the sole ownership of the curriculum, or that it is even desirable to think that we are the only ones who should be calling the shots. My uncertainty has nothing to do with an orally-based language program. I still believe in that. Rather, this uncertainty stems from the fact that the world around us has changed in the fifteen years that I have been teaching Japanese at the university level.

There are at least two factors for my uncertainty, one internal to the field of the Japanese teaching profession and the other external. To mention the conclusion first, these factors point to a curriculum design that must be flexible in content. These factors suggest models for teaching that, in some cases, call on colleagues in other disciplines to assist with at least a part of the curriculum. That is, a joint ownership of the curriculum instead of the traditional sole ownership model. I'll begin with the internal factor.

The Japanese language profession has had a virtually monogamous relationship with the field of literature. This is not limited to Japanese, but it is true of most foreign languages. Looking back on the history of the development of Japanese studies in this country, it is somewhat odd that this relationship between language teaching and literature was begun in the first place. One of the biggest incentives for the study of Japanese was World War II, and subsequently, eminent scholars such as Edwin Reischauer sustained interest in the study of Japanese. So why did Japanese language teaching fall together with literature? As far as I can see, this was simply following the academic convention in this country that traditionally places modern languages together with literary studies. According to a colleague in German studies, this academic tradition can be traced back to the old German academic model. In this model, literature is the study of the classics. Modern languages are viewed as an extension of the classic languages, often poor and imperfect extensions. Hence the study of modern languages was put into literature departments, with literary studies being the primary goal of the language program. In this model, the study of modern languages is secondary to the study of literature and classical languages. When modern Japanese was introduced into the curriculum in this country, it was this traditional model that was followed. So, in virtually all institutions, study of modern Japanese takes place in some sort of language and literature program. The same is true of most other foreign languages. In this conventional academic context, the goal of the language program is naturally geared to the dominant content-focus of the department, that of literature. The goal becomes the ability to read the national literature of Japan. Even in the orally-based program I designed with colleagues at Ohio State, it was literature that topped off the language program at the time.

The factor internal to the field that is contributing to my uncertainty about the ownership of the language curriculum has to do with the fact that the nature of literary studies has changed fundamentally in the past fifteen years or so. The concept of "cultural studies" is quickly replacing the traditional "literary studies" as the primary intellectual endeavor for humanistic studies. The change in the name of some departments from "language and literature" to "language and culture" is but one reflection of this fundamental shift. Here's the challenge. If you look at cultural studies, it is easy to see that virtually nothing—in fact nothing—is excluded from a potential subject matter of study. Research in cultural studies may take on world music, post-colonial societies, or even the very nature of scientific revolution. It also includes what we might call traditional literary studies, although it is common to question even the very concept of a literary text. In this context, in a typical language program that has literature as the culmination of the program, it is no longer certain exactly what content we are supposed to provide, particularly at the advanced level. We have been claiming ownership of a language program commonly with traditional literary studies as the primary goal. But in the face of what is happening in cultural studies, this ownership seems virtually a moot point. The question before us is what content should a language program have at the upper levels? Particularly given the interdisciplinary nature of cultural studies, which encompasses a broad range of subject matter, there is a real possibility that the content-focus of the language curriculum will likely include studies outside the traditional language and literature domain. The boundaries that encapsulated traditional literary studies are breaking down. The language and literature faculty will no longer be able to claim sole ownership of the language curriculum. This is the internal factor for my uncertainty.

Turning to the external factor contributing to my uncertainty, as I mentioned above, the field of Japanese language has had for the most part a monogamous relationship. Internally, it has been with literature, which has been the goal of most programs, although, as I just mentioned, it is no longer clear who our partner is anymore. I believe that, external to the field, our most common partner has been with business, in that at many institutions, there have been more students in business taking Japanese than from any other field of study. This seems incongruous—carrying on a relationship internally with literature for content, and externally with business, by teaching large numbers of business students. But that is simply an historical accident, in which the tradition of literature-focused language curriculum met the demand of business in the 1980s and into the 1990s. The 1991 MLA statistics showed that between 1986 and 1990, the enrollment in Japanese at the college level in this country virtually doubled, reaching almost 45,000 students. Two earlier MLA surveys, in 1983 and 1986, also showed that Japanese was the fastest growing foreign language. This rapid expansion has a reason independent of Japanese studies. The enormous increase mirrors directly the growth in business enrollment. In the second half of the 1980s, there were more students majoring in business in this country than in any other field of study. But in the 1990s, the number of business students has stabilized, and in some cases this number had decreased. This has likewise contributed to the stabilizing of enrollment in Japanese. Combined with the recession in Japan, this trend has led to a decrease in Japanese enrollment in some institutions. Thus, Japanese programs are no longer going to be overwhelmingly dominated by business majors. Instead, we are beginning to see a more diverse group of learners. These learners come from a variety of disciplines, leading again to the question, what content should we provide for the language curriculum?

I have laid out two assumptions. The field of literary studies, which has dominated the focus of Japanese language education, is being transformed into cultural studies, which embraces a broad approach to humanistic studies. This is a factor internal to the field. Externally, our clientele is changing—it is no longer primarily business. This is where I see our profession today: we are uncertain about both internal and external factors that affect our field. I don't have the confidence I had fifteen years ago in the belief that the faculty of the language and literature department should hold the sole ownership of the Japanese language curriculum.

What is happening in the field now as a result of these and related changes? One phenomenon, still restricted in number, is that we are beginning to see multiple Japanese programs on one campus. I am told, for example, that at a major institution on the east coast, there are three Japanese language programs, one in the traditional language and literature department, another at a center for modern languages, and yet a third in the business school. At another institution, along with the language program in the East Asian department, the School of Engineering started its own Japanese program. This phenomenon is in part a reaction to the fact that the traditional, literature-based program does not serve today's students. This is the result of the incongruous relationship between literature content and the practical needs of students in business, engineering, and other professional schools. The phenomenon of offering an independent Japanese program in the engineering and business schools also reflects the external factor. There is a diversification of learner clientele, and at these schools, it was apparently deemed necessary to offer a Japanese program geared to students in specific fields of study, such as business or engineering. This trend points to a multiple ownership of the Japanese curriculum at one institution: the language and literature faculty holding on to the ownership of its own literature-focused program, and a new program whose ownership lies with the language specialists in a professional school.

How should we deal with this trend of multiple ownership as a field? Should we embrace it or reject it? In thinking about the institutional context for this issue, it is helpful to think of two other disciplines that, in style, are at opposite extremes. These are mathematics and statistics. Students who need to take math go to the mathematics department. In other words, the mathematics faculty hold the sole ownership of the mathematics curriculum. Statistics is often fundamentally different. Particularly in a large institution, we find statistics courses taught in different programs: mathematics, psychology, and education, for example. Statistics is therefore taught across a variety of curricula in accordance with the specific needs of a particular field.

How about foreign languages? The dominant model is the same as mathematics. Students who want to study Japanese come to the language and literature department. However, what we are seeing at institutions such as those I mentioned earlier reflects the model established for statistics — Japanese for specific use.

Regardless of the uncertainty of the times, one thing I am absolutely certain of is that those of us in the teaching profession possess the pedagogical expertise that must be the basis for any reputable language curriculum. Whether there is sole ownership or multiple ownership of the language curriculum at an institution, what we must avoid is the creation of language programs that are questionable in the quality of training they offer. At the same time, the forces at play are great, and we cannot underestimate how rapidly this ownership of pedagogical expertise can be overshadowed by institutional politics and economy. If a school of management decides that the language program offered in the language and literature department fails to meet the needs of its students, then the school will have the financial and political resources to start a program of its own. But the faculty of management schools do not possess expertise in language teaching. We should not stand still and allow non-experts to take away, or fragment, the ownership of the language curriculum. Of this I am certain. As far as I can see, this has not happened yet, but as resources become scarce, the temptation to offer language courses on the cheap will become great.

It is important to emphasize that I count literature specialists who teach language as critical members of the language teaching profession. My uncertainty about the sole focus of literature as content is independent of the areas of specialization of the teaching profession. I know of a number of excellent teachers of Japanese whose specialization is literature. They are pedagogy specialists whose teaching skills match, and often exceed, the standard we have maintained in the field. I am simply questioning the dominance of literature as the content for language programs. I would have a similar question if the dominant content of an advanced course were linguistics, for example. But this issue is independent of the ability of the linguists in the field to teach language. The teaching profession consists of those who have a commitment to offering an excellent program in Japanese, regardless of their area of specialization. Also, it is important to emphasize that I am by no means advocating excluding literature from Japanese language programs. In certain instances, traditional literary studies may very well be the appropriate content focus. Other programs may incorporate literature in varying degrees, depending on its appropriateness to the curriculum and student interest.

But how do we ensure that the teaching profession will continue to hold ownership of at least the *standard* of education? Let me suggest two broad areas where we must put in work. Both call for strong leadership in the profession. We must play a proactive role in our own institutions. We can no longer afford to sit still and play the passive observer in academe. We have been lucky that our enrollment has increased dramatically, giving us the base to expand and enhance our position in our institutions. This has happened in the 1980s without much effort to recruit students. If anything, many of us discouraged students from taking Japanese in order to control the overflow. Now it is time to become proactive. It is more important than ever to build necessary bridges with disciplines across the curriculum, may it be management, engineering, social sciences, or whatever. Do we adopt the mathematics model or the across-the-curriculum statistics model? That will depend on the local conditions and the individual style of the leadership of the language program. In either case, we must be willing to move away from the Japanese-solely-for-literature model that persists in the majority of the language programs in the U.S. We must be prepared, if necessary, to give up a part of the ownership of the language curriculum in order to better serve the diverse group of students we see, and also in order to ensure that those of us in the teaching profession continue to hold the ownership of the *standard* of education. Here is a point worth noting. Most of the faculty, particularly senior faculty, who are in the most influential positions to mold the future of the Japanese language curriculum are literature specialists. But I am claiming that the traditional literature paradigm for language learning is insufficient, both internal and external to the field. So, I appeal particularly to my senior literature colleagues to exert leadership in this time of uncertainty. A proactive attitude is needed both to ensure the quality of language education and to better serve a wider range of students. Let me note a point made by John Grandin, a Kafka scholar of German who designed a part of the University of Rhode Island German program to meet the needs of the engineering students. By refocusing the German program, he and his colleagues reversed the downward trend for enrollment. Not only is the enrollment up considerably in the basic levels, but it is also up in the literature courses that in the past often failed to make the cut. So, moving away from the monolithic literature paradigm may in fact help the literature enrollment.

What is it that we must do as a field? The bottom line is that we must be willing to be flexible in the kinds of content we offer and even in the way we deliver instruction. We can no longer justify language teaching primarily as a preparation for the study of the national literature of Japan. If literature is not the goal, then exactly what is the goal of a language curriculum? As John Grandin, et al. (1992) write, it is imperative that we adopt the view that a foreign language is "a communication tool to facilitate other areas of study, of which literature is just one example" (129). This view, once taken, has broad consequences for the design of the curriculum. First, regardless of the area of study, the students require a robust set of skills in speaking and listening. One change that has occurred in the past fifteen years is that people have become highly mobile. Regardless of whether you are in business or academics, people are coming in direct contact with each other more than ever before. The need for speaking and listening is obvious. What is not so obvious is that this requirement for speaking and listening may very well hold even when interacting with people other than those from Japan. I was told of a meeting on Japanese that took place in Japan that was attended by people from all over the world. A professor who was asked to lecture to the group had prepared her talk in English, but as it turned out, the one common language shared by everyone was Japanese, so she ended up lecturing in Japanese. Granted this was a meeting on Japanese. However, one can foresee in the near future situations like this in business, for example, where the common language is Japanese, particularly in parts of Asia. Just as the U.S. dollar is being questioned in some quarters as the international currency, with the Japanese yen being mentioned as a possible alternative, it is possible that the international language in some parts of the world may become Japanese.

The second consequence of adopting the view that foreign language training is primarily a communication tool to facilitate study of other areas concerns the content focus of the curriculum. In this regard, it is instructive to see what the professionals in other languages are doing to meet the challenge of a diverse group of learners. A number of institutions are experimenting with what is commonly called foreign languages across the curriculum. The proponents of foreign languages across the curriculum, or FLAC, believe that more students will be motivated to continue their study into the upper levels if the content is of direct relevance to their own area of specialization. FLAC may be implemented in a number of different ways, but they all share the common feature that the students have an opportunity to study their own area at least partly in the target language. A common FLAC model identifies faculty members in other departments who are speakers of the target language and collaborates with them to establish a curriculum. This is shared ownership of the language curriculum, one that takes into account the assumption that a foreign language is a tool for communication. This is the kind of model I rebelled against fifteen years ago. Granted, this is more easily accomplished in the European languages, which allow authentic materials to be introduced at an earlier stage of training, than for a language such as Japanese. But we cannot use this as an excuse for not being proactive. At MIT, for example, we plan to experiment with the use of technology to compensate for the level of difficulty, by producing on-line software assistance for students at upper levels who want to study Japanese through material directly pertinent to their area of study, such as genetics, material science, and economics. The challenge before us is great. It can only be met with strong leadership and a willingness to build bridges with other areas of study. And to allow for the possibility that we might have to share ownership of the language curriculum with colleagues in other disciplines.

The final point I wish to make has to do with our national organization, the Association of Teachers of Japanese. Articles published in the ATJ journal are primarily on literature, with a sprinkling of linguistics. There is a dearth of publications that relate directly to language teaching.[2] The preponderance of literature articles sustains the traditional view of the language program as primarily serving the field of literature.[3] ATJ has served our field well up to this point, thanks to the effective leadership of its presidents, Hiroshi Miyaji, Jim O'Brien, Eleanor Jorden, and others who preceded them. But now the field faces a time of uncertainty, and I call on the ATJ to exert leadership at the national level, as we make the transition from a traditional literature-based curriculum to one that serves a broad range of learners. The most important thing for us as a field is to communicate with each other more extensively in order to keep abreast of the emerging trends in learner interest, second language acquisition, and curricular development. ATJ can play an important role at the national level in disseminating information with broad pedagogical interests through publication in its journal. An equally important effort is to continue to encourage national and regional meetings where this type of information can be shared.

To sum up, we have a great deal of work to do. We are in a time of transition as a field, a time of uncertainty. With strong leadership both at the institutional and national levels, I am confident that we will continue to hold much of the ownership of the language curriculum and the standard of quality, although we must face the real possibility that we should begin to share some of the ownership of the curriculum with colleagues from other fields of study, in order to ensure that the Japanese language will continue to play a vibrant role on our campuses.

Notes

1. I am using the term "owner" to refer to those who have the primary jurisdiction and leadership of the curriculum.
2. I have been informed by an ATJ Board member that the primary reason for the lack of articles on language teaching in the JATJ is that manuscripts in pedagogy tend to be lower in quality than those in literature or linguistics. If this is indeed the case, we must find ways to enhance the quality of work in pedagogy. A natural way to do this is to continue to hold national and regional conferences on language education in which abstracts are refereed. This will establish a national standard of work in pedagogy maintained by the leaders in the field who take part in the referee process.
3. There are three encouraging exceptions. ATJ will publish the proceedings of the national conference on Japanese language teaching held at Georgetown University in April 1995. Also, an upcoming issue of the Journal of the Association of Teachers of Japanese will focus on linguistics. Finally, for the past two years, ATJ has sponsored or cosponsored a national conference on language teaching, at MIT in March 1994 and at Georgetown University in April 1995.

Reference

Grandin, J., K. Einbeck, and W. Von Reinhart. 1992. "The Changing Goals of Language Instruction." In *Languages for a Multicultural World in Transition*, Ed. Heidi Byrnes, 123-163. Middlebury, VT: Northeast Conference on the Teaching of Foreign Languages.

SHAPING CURRICULUM

Transparency of Curriculum

Mari Noda

1. Introduction: The Players of Curriculum

1.1 Definition of Curriculum

In a coherent program of instruction, we expect or hope to have a defined manner of progression of instruction from the beginning to the advanced levels. To guide us through these progressions, we establish a curriculum. A foreign language curriculum can be defined as the organization of what to do and how to do it in order for teachers to teach and students to learn the target language within a formal institutionalized setting (Lang 1990).

1.2. The Players

Since it is usually the teachers who establish the curriculum in a given program, we tend to see curriculum as the guidelines for teachers. However, there is another player implied in the definition of curriculum. To see that, we can rephrase the definition of curriculum given above to read that it is the organization of what *teachers and students* are to do and how to do it, in order for teachers to teach and students to learn the target language. A teacher creates the curriculum, but if learners enact it as much as teachers, how do we convey to the learners the organizational principles we call curriculum? And how much of the curricular information do we give to our students? These are all questions I want to address. In other words, I want to discuss the transparency of curriculum to students in Japanese language programs.

2. Stating the Curriculum

2.1. The Syllabus as a Place for the Overt Statement of Curriculum

There are a number of things through which learners detect what they are to do and how they are to do it. The textbooks and other materials they are told to use, the presentation of the materials in the learning materials, the speed with which the materials are covered, the kind of activities in which they engage both in the classroom and at home, and the ways in which their learning is evaluated. But the only overt means through which teachers convey to learners what to do, how to do it, and why, is the set of course syllabi used in the program.

In the present climate of encouraging learner-centered instruction, extremists might say that students should be involved in the creation of curriculum.[1] But there is a fundamental problem in such a claim. It is the assumption that learners are best equipped to design their learning. Teachers are, we hope, trained to teach. Some are both trained and experienced.[2] By the time individuals reach high-school age, they have had a lot of experience in learning. However, experience alone does not make them better learners. As Hammerly (1985) puts it, practice makes not perfect, but practice makes permanent. In addition, the mode of learning is strongly influenced by the cultural definitions of what learning is. American learners tend to learn to reason and present individual argumentation, while Japanese learners tend to learn to intake and remember facts that are given. Neither group, especially the American group, typically equate learning with model imitation, synthesis, trial, and adjustment, all of which are essential to language learning. In fact, in both cultures, only a small portion of what the learners already know about language learning is directly applicable to what they will have to do in order to learn a foreign language. We cannot assume that the average student has the ability to extract what to do and how to do it from the teacher's choice of instructional materials or the teacher's methodology. An explicit statement is needed, and the most logical place to present it is in the course syllabus.

2.2. Rationale for Having the Syllabus

If the program is not institutionalized, a course syllabus may not be necessary. The teacher and the student can have a verbal agreement of their respective responsibilities, and not bother with a written statement about a course syllabus. In an institutionalized setting, there are several reasons for having a written syllabus.

First, having a written syllabus helps coordinate the teachers and students in multiple-section courses. The situation at The Ohio State University (OSU) might be considered to be at the opposite end of the scale from the intimate situation mentioned above. The first-level, first-quarter course taught during the academic year typically starts out with about 160 students divided into eight sections. Several teachers collaborate in teaching a single course. A general agreement among teachers and among students is as important as that between the teaching team, on the one hand, and the students, on the other hand. A "case-by-case" method does not work in this size of program. More important, however, is the programmatic cohesion that having a set of coordinated course syllabi can permit. Every Japanese language course offered at OSU is regarded as part of the program that can last as long as four years for any given student. A student taking Japanese 101 commits not only to ten weeks of study of Japanese, but, potentially, to 120 weeks of classes. Once the fifth level is created as planned, students will potentially have as much as 150 weeks, or 830 class hours, of instruction. Even those who are only taking Japanese to fulfill their language requirement have to take it for forty weeks over four quarters. It is only fair that students at the beginning are given some idea of where they are going and what they will have to do to get there.

The third reason for having a written curriculum description applies only to higher education. It has to do with an increasing number of students who choose colleges based on the Japanese program offered. This is a happy trend. The national survey of Japanese programs in this country (Jorden and Lambert 1991) indicates that even though a large number of students taking Japanese in high schools are college-bound and intend to continue their studies of Japanese at the college level, very few of them state that they would look at the Japanese programs in selecting the colleges to which they apply.[3] In the last two years, we have begun to have inquiries, mostly from parents of high school students, about our Japanese program. Those who call us say that they are considering schools that have good reputations in their Japanese programs. They want to know what exactly we offer. For these students, the transparency of the curriculum will be a major determining factor not just in their choice of courses once they begin college study, but in their choice of the place of higher education.

3. Syllabus Content

3.1. Statement of Responsibilities in Curriculum Management

Once a curriculum is implemented, it has to be enacted and managed. Both the teacher, or the team of teachers, and learners are responsible for the management of the curriculum. Course syllabi can serve as the statement of the curriculum through the assignment of responsibilities in managing the curriculum. It is in this sense that the analogy between course syllabi and service contracts become possible. The fundamental difference between these documents is that the course syllabus is not negotiated by the two parties, the teacher and the student, the way service contracts normally are.

Given the goals and the local conditions of the program, curriculum is the means through which teachers and learners reach the stated goals. The syllabus is a documentation of the players' respective responsibilities in managing the curriculum. Figure 1 captures the relationship between program goals, curriculum, and local conditions.

The statement of curriculum need not include all of the instructional principles listed in NFLC's Curricular Framework (1993). Rather, it should focus on what the learners can expect from the teachers and what responsibilities they will have as learners.

Shaping Curriculum

```
                    ┌─────────────────────────┐
                    │         GOALS           │
                    └─────────────────────────┘
                          ▲             ▲
                    T                         S
                          CURRICULUM
    • Set up context                    • Work with tapes
    • Check performance                 • Memorize
    • Provide help                      • Perform

                    ┌─────────────────────────────────────────┐
                    │           LOCAL CONDITIONS              │
                    │ e.g. • Setting • Motivation • Teacher/Student Ratio │
                    └─────────────────────────────────────────┘
```

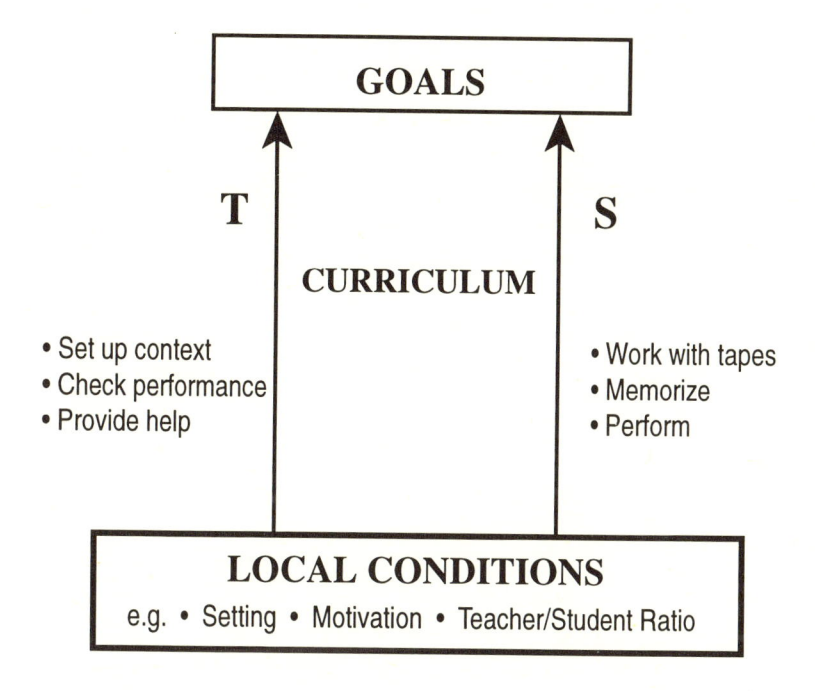

Figure 1: Syllabus connecting goals and local conditions in a language program

3.2. Local Conditions

Local conditions are a given, and, therefore, don't need to be stated in the syllabus. Local conditions may include such factors as the physical setting of the school and the classroom, type of students, student motivation, teacher/student ratio, length of a class, the frequency of the class, class/preparation time ratio for teachers and students, institutional support of the language program, etc. These are the ingredients with which one has to work in creating and managing the curriculum. Attempts have been made in NFLC's Curricular Framework as well as in the State of Washington's Communicative Framework (Brockett et al. 1994) to describe a setup that is most conducive to optimum curriculum implementation. The reality in some locales remains harsher than the optimum.

3.3. Program Goals

In an ideal program, the program goals match perfectly with the goals of the learners. In most institutions such a perfect match is an impossibility simply due to the diverse goals students bring to a single program. It is, of course, desirable to have the learners' goals reflected in establishing the program goals. Program goals are not necessarily a given, but they are predetermined before curriculum is designed, and they need to be stated in the syllabus to set the context of the creation of the particular curriculum. Goals are frequently different from the outcome of instruction. The curriculum is constantly adjusted to minimize the gap between the preestablished goals and the observed outcome of the program. In other words, the curriculum is negotiated.

4. A Sample Syllabus

4.1. Introduction to the Program

I want to offer as a basis of future discussion a course syllabus I have used at The Ohio State University. Every learner who is new to the Japanese program at OSU is given two things to get them started. These are the "Introduction to Japanese at OSU," which contains information that is relevant at any level of instruction within the Japanese language program (see Appendix A); and they are also given a text called "How to Work with Tapes." Finally, each student is asked to fill out a "Background Questionnaire" that becomes the basis for a file containing any information relevant to the student's studies in Japanese. This file is kept until the student leaves the program.

The first key item in "Introduction to Japanese at OSU" is the statement of long-term goals toward which the OSU program strives. It outlines the means through which the objectives are achieved, especially in the first three and a half levels of instruction. These include informal interaction in Japanese with the instructional staff, the formal sessions that are divided into ACT and FACT sessions, and the self-managed work. It also provides general information about the location of language labs and their hours of operation.

In levels one through three, and part of level four, daily grading is adopted. A scale of 0 to 4 is used, and each score is explained in terms of performance in the "Introduction" document. While daily grading is a useful device for progress assessment and continuous feedback, without a clear explanation of what the numbers mean, students assume that it is a purely subjective, and therefore, unfair system of grade assignment. Also, students should receive a report of the daily grades they are getting at regular intervals throughout the course, so that the feedback is continuous.

Students often try to translate the daily grading score to a letter grade, so the relationship between daily grades and a letter grade is provided as a guideline, in order to maintain consistency in the formula at all levels of instruction and among all teaching staff of the program.

4.2. Course Syllabus

For each course, there is a course-specific syllabus. As an example, Appendix B is a syllabus that was used for intermediate intensive courses offered in Autumn Quarter, 1994. These courses accelerate the study of Japanese by doubling the class hours. In one academic year, they cover materials equivalent to those covered in two or three regular-track courses.

The general purpose of the course is stated first in terms of where the course fits into the overall program, and students are referred to the general "Introduction to Japanese at OSU" for information about the program objectives. The syllabus states the name(s) of the instructor(s) and their office location(s). A syllabus would also typically state the intended type of student by identifying the target population and the limiting factors in terms of prerequisites. In this course syllabus, a prerequisite is not specifically mentioned because the computerized registration system enforces prerequisites.

Because the course objectives are to be interpreted within the context of the long-term objectives stated in "Introduction to Japanese at OSU," the individual course syllabus includes only course-specific objectives stated in terms of what the learners will become able to do. These include such areas as interaction strategies they can learn to use, types of text they will read and write, and acquisition strategies they will practice.

The general introduction to the program indicates what the learners are supposed to do in formal and self-managed settings. The specific tasks related to particular course materials are outlined in the schedule of ACT sessions provided along with the syllabus. (See Appendix C, for example.) The weekly schedule refers to the ACT session number assigned to specific tasks for which students are responsible in each ACT class session. This ensures that students will know the weight of each task for which they are responsible in the curriculum management. And since this is a performance-oriented course, the grading of daily performance has the largest weight. This makes it necessary for the instructor to provide continuous feedback in the form of a weekly report on daily performance scores.

The more heavily the daily performance scores count toward the course grade, the more crucial it becomes to state the provisions for unavoidable absences. Make-up sessions can be scheduled regardless of the reason for the absence, up to a specified number of classes. The policy statements provide the restrictions that apply to this basic mechanism through which students are encouraged to actually make up the practice they might have missed. There is no need to spend the time listening to the cause of the absence or debate as to whether or not the reason given is a good excuse. Also, students will not miss the instructional session altogether from absences. Since they have to prepare for the make-up session in addition to preparing for the regular classes scheduled on the make-up date, students do not abuse the system either.

4.3. Follow-Up and "Spiraling"

Students will not always remember their responsibilities in the joint venture of curriculum enactment, even if they are stated clearly in the course syllabus, unless they are reminded of them regularly. That does not mean the clear statement isn't necessary. It is important for students to know what they are agreeing to do when they enroll in a course. This is especially true in schools where students enroll in courses selectively. What is important is that the stated elements of goals and curriculum for reaching them have to be repeated a number of times in different contexts in the course of the term.

5. Conclusion

Giving learners an overall picture of the program helps them manage the curriculum successfully. Both the multiple number of teachers, including graduate teaching assistants, and the learners share a similar understanding of what is required of them in the learning process. Having to explicate the required tasks and the manner in which these tasks are to be completed also helps the instructor in charge have a clearer understanding of the shaping of the curriculum.

APPENDIX A: Introduction to a Language Program

Introduction to Japanese at OSU, DEALL

Welcome to the Japanese program in the Department of East Asian Languages and Literatures (DEALL) at The Ohio State University. Here is some important information about our Japanese language program.

Long-Term Objective of a Foreign Language Learner:

You will become able to participate in activities within the target culture, using the target language, through development of long-term associations with the people of that culture. This will require the ability to express oneself in a culturally appropriate manner and to understand the intentions of the natives from their behavior, including their speech.

Objectives in Specific Courses:

See course introductions.

Means:

1. Informal interactions:
    The "official language" of the program is Japanese whenever there is a Japanese-speaking participant in the conversation. Remember that Japanese is not just a language you practice in class, but a way of being and acting with other people. Take advantage of the presence of those who are Japanese speakers, and interact with them in Japanese.
2. Formal session: ("classes")
    There are two types of classes: ACT classes and FACT classes.
2.1. ACT classes:
    These are the core of the program since it is in ACT classes that you practice using the language to communicate and to interact with Japanese people. You will practice handling various realistic situations using Japanese. A score will be given for each ACT class based on your performance. (See rating description on the last page.)
2.2. FACT classes:
    FACT classes, conducted mainly in English, are about Japanese and learning Japanese. They support the ACT classes by dealing with grammatical and sociocultural aspects of Japanese, as well as your strategies for learning Japanese. You will have the opportunity to ask questions in English. Obviously, the more advanced you are, the fewer FACT classes you will need.
3. Self-managed work:
3.1. Audio tapes:
    You are expected to work with the JSL audio tapes both in the Listening Center and at home. We recommend that you do your tape work at one of the Listening Centers, since there will be fewer distractions there than at home.
3.2. Homework:
    The Listening Center allows you to make copies of JSL tapes for home use. You should allocate time to work on JSL tapes at home, especially during weekends when the Lab is closed.

Media Centers:

You will work extensively with audio and video materials available for use in the following media centers. (Hours may change from quarter to quarter.) Audio tapes may be duplicated there.

- Cunz 108 M-Th 8 am - 7 pm; F 8 am - 5 pm.
- Denney 060 M-Th 8 am - 9 pm; F 8 am - 5 pm; Sn 2-9 pm

GRADING POLICY STATEMENT

The Japanese language program at OSU uses the scoring of daily performance as its key means of evaluating student achievement. In every class hour in which you are expected to perform in Japanese, i.e., ACT hour, you will be evaluated with a score ranging from 0 to 4, according to the following scale.

4.0 Performance showed no obstacle to communication.
3.5 Performance showed a noticeable obstacle to communication.
3.0 Performance showed more that one obstacle to communication, and communication was achieved with a little effort on the part of the instructor or interlocutor.
2.5 Performance showed more than one obstacle to communication, and communication was achieved only with substantial effort on the part of the instructor and interlocutor.
2.0 Performance showed multiple obstacles to communication, but with substantial correction and guidance on the part of the instructor or interlocutor, communication was achieved.
1.5 Performance showed multiple obstacles to communication. Partial communication was achieved with persistent correction and guidance from instructor or interlocutor.
1.0 "Warm-body" point: attended class, but could not demonstrate any appreciable degree of preparation or understanding.
0   Absent.

These scores do not correspond to the grade-to-number relationship used by the University to calculate the GPA. Rather, the average of your daily performance grade will be converted to a percentage using 4.0 as 100%, and this will be combined with percentage scores from the evaluation of other activities to determine the course grade. The combined percentage is usually interpreted according to the following scale.

100% to 87.5%	A to A-
87.4% to 75%	B+ to B-
74.9% to 62.5%	C+ to C-
62.4% to 50%	D+ to D
Lower than 50%	E

APPENDIX B: Sample Course Syllabus

Japanese 210/211 (OSU DEALL) Fall 1994

Introduction

Okaeri-nasai. "Welcome back!"
The purpose of this course is to develop further the foundation of Japanese that you have built in Japanese 101 through 103. If you did not take Japanese 103 at OSU during Spring or Summer quarter, 1994, see your instructor for placement testing. Refer to "Introduction to Japanese at OSU" for information about program objectives, instructional design, and general grading policies.

The following information is specific to this course.

Faculty:
Professor Mari NODA, 156B Cunz (292-2214)
Professor Charles J. QUINN Jr., 185 Cunz (292-0186)

Graduate Teaching Assistant:
Ms. Shinko KAGAYA, 486 Cunz (292-9537)

Office hours: to be announced

Rooms:
8:30 (210) = Central Classroom 245; 9:30 = Denney 358

Course Objectives (specific goals for this quarter):
In 210 and 211, you will

1. review, refine, and reinforce Japanese interactional strategies practiced in Japanese 101-103;
2. gain skills for interactions that involve explaining, complaining, telephoning, introducing, making speculations, comparing, and expressing change of state;
3 expand your ability to read and write simple memos and messages using katakana, hiragana, and kanji; and
4. develop basic strategies to learn more Japanese through actual interaction.

Learning Materials:
- *Japanese: The Spoken Language Part 1* and *Part 2* (Jorden/Noda) = JSL 1 and JSL 2 (available at SBX)
- JSL 2 video cassette tape (available at SBX)
- JSL 1 Question and Answer Supplement (available at SBX)
- JSL audio tapes (available in the Media Centers) JPN09 series for JSL 1, JPN08 for JSL 2.

The audio tapes for JSL 2 are somewhat different from the audio tapes for JSL 1. You will have to use the pause/stop and rewind buttons extensively since there are no pauses or reverse buildup of CCs in the tapes. Be sure to work with the appropriate drills in order to practice the additional and supplementary vocabulary. There is no separate section for Breakdown.
Bring good-quality 90-minute tapes in order to duplicate the tapes, unless you plan to work with tapes in the tape lab.

- *Japanese: The Written Language Part 1 Field Test Edition* (Jorden/Noda) = JWL 1 (available at SBX) and JWL 2 (available at Grade A Notes later in the quarter)
- Handouts

Evaluation and Grading:
- Same grades will be given for 210 and 211.
- Your course grade will be determined by the following criteria:

    Daily Performance Score (0-4 in every ACT hour)   60%
    Midterm Examination   15%
    Quiz scores   15%
    Homework scores   10%

- See Introduction to Japanese at OSU for daily grading criteria. Feel free to ask about your scores after ACT classes. You will receive a report on your scores weekly starting in Week Two. It is your responsibility to examine each report carefully and report any errors to the instructor immediately.

Make-Up Policies:
- *If you miss an ACT class*, you may make it up regardless of your reason for the absence. Observe the following.

    (1) You may make up a maximum of six class hours for the two courses combined.

    (2) You must make up the missed class *within three days* (excluding weekends and holidays) after your return. If you miss two consecutive days, the first of the two days must be made up within three days upon your return, the second day within four days.

    (3) It is your responsibility to schedule an appointment with any of the instructors who taught the hour you missed. If there are multiple sections, this need not be the teacher who taught your own section.

    (4) Since no questions will be asked about the reason for your absence, it will not be necessary for you to present any documents explaining your absence (e.g. medical excuses, job-related assignments).

    (5) Each make-up session will last no longer than five minutes.

    (6) You will receive a performance score for each make-up session and this will become your daily performance score for the hour that you missed.

(7) *No make-up sessions* may be scheduled in Weeks Ten and Eleven.
- If you miss a quiz, the percentage score for the first quiz you take after your return will be counted twice. This will apply to *ONE* quiz only, but not if you miss the last scheduled quiz.
- The midterm *examination may not be made up.*
- Late *homework* will be accepted for up to one week after the due date. However, there will be a penalty of 5% of the score for each day it is late. No homework turned in after the last day of classes will count toward your course grade.

APPENDIX C: Sample of ACT Sessions

JSL stands for *Japanese: The Spoken Language*
JWL stands for *Japanese: The Written Language*

ACT Session 1 JSL Introduction
Classroom Instructions (="CI")
Greetings and Useful Phrases (="GUP") #1, 2, 3, 4, 5
Preview: GUP #18, 19; 14, 15, 20
Follow the instructor.

For the next and all following ACT sessions, you should come prepared to PERFORM smoothly, accurately, and to the best of your knowledge of the Japanese way of doing things (as described in JSL). Language is dead outside of its cultural context.

ACT Session 2 GUP
GUP: #18, 19; 14, 15, 20
Review: CI and previously introduced GUP
Preview: GUP #6, 7, 8; 12, 13; 17

To prepare for this session, listen to tape #0 in JPN 09 series. Practice the GUPs by repeating them until you can say them smoothly. Pay careful attention to their meanings. Go over How to Work with Tapes.

Your instructor will provide context in which it is appropriate to say the phrases you have prepared to say. Try to learn the association between context and speech. You should be learning not only how to say something in Japanese, but also when to say what.

Do not repeat the CI phrases, but be able to respond to them with appropriate action.

ACT Session 3 GUP
GUP #6, 7, 8; 12, 13; 17
Review: CI and GUP previously introduced.
Preview: GUP #9, 10, 11; 16, 1A
Continue to work with Tape #0. Follow instructions on How to Work with Tapes. But also start listening to Tape(s) for JSL 1.

Now we will start the Lessons in JSL.

"1A" = JSL Lesson 1, Section A.
"CC" = Core Conversation

Remember that you are to come to class ready to perform the designated CC for the day.

ACT Session 4 GUP/JSL 1A
GUP #9, 10, 11; 16,
Review: all GUP and CI
Preview: CC 1, 2, 3, 4
ACT Session 5 JSL 1A
CC Performance: CC 1, 2, 3, 4
Review: GUP and CI
Preview: CC 5, 6, 7, 8, 9, 10
Are you following the instructions in How to Work with Tapes when you practice your CCs ?

"Drills": You will find drills in the JSL Tapes as well as in the textbook. Rely first on the tapes, and use textbook only to check what you hear. Practice activities in class will require that you have worked on these drills thoroughly, but the classroom activities do not replicate what you can do using the tapes. With the tapes, you should practice responding to cues until you are able to do so automatically while knowing what you are *doing* by saying what you say. Always think about whether you are agreeing, inviting, requesting, accepting, and so forth.

ACT Session 6 JSL 1A
CC Performance: CC 5, 6, 7, 8
Review CC 1-4
Drill: A, B, C (Tape JPN 09 #1A2)

Now is the time to pay close attention to your pronunciation. As you go on, you will be preparing more and more complex things for each session so that it will be difficult to spend time on pronunciation. Also, the longer you practice with imperfect pronunciation, the greater the chance of your solidifying that imperfect pronunciation.

ACT Session 7 JSL 1A
CC Performance: CC 9, 10
Drills: D, E, F, G
Review all CCs in 1A
Application Exercise: A3

To prepare for the Application Exercises, you should review the CCs and/or the Drills which contain the patterns and vocabulary you need. This means more work with tapes. Aim for fluency. How is your pronunciation? Are you working with tapes?

Notes

1. Nunan (1988) asserts that learner-centered curriculum differs from "traditional" curriculum development in that "in the former, the curriculum is a collaborative effort between teachers and learners, since learners are closely involved in the decision-making process regarding the content of the curriculum and how it is taught" (2).
2. And many, alas, are experienced, but not trained.
3. Of the 1,142 sample high school students studying Japanese, 5.6% said that they are expecting to continue studying Japanese in college. But more than one third of them plan to major in applied and professional subjects (e.g. business). Given choices, they are more likely to choose schools with good programs in business, for example, rather than looking into the quality of the Japanese program in prospective schools.

References

Brockett, Chris and Leslie Okada Birkland, et al. 1994. *A Communicative Framework for Introductory Japanese Language Curricula in Washington State High Schools.* Olympia, WA: Office of Superintendent of Public Instruction.

Hammerly, Hector. 1985. *An Integrated Theory of Language Teaching and Its Practical Consequences.* Blaine, WA: Second Language Publications.

Jorden, Eleanor H. and Richard D. Lambert. 1991. *Japanese Language Instruction in the United States: Resources, Practice, and Investment Strategy.* Washington DC: National Foreign Language Center.

Lang, Dale. 1990. "Sketching the Crisis and Exploring Different Perspectives in Foreign Language Curriculum." In *New Perspectives and New Directions in Foreign Language Education*, Ed. Diane W. Birckbichler, 77-109. Lincolnwood: National Textbook Company.

Nunan, David. 1988. *The Learner-Centered Curriculum.* Cambridge: Cambridge University Press.

Unger, J. Marshall et al. 1993. *A Framework for Introductory Japanese Language Curricula in American High Schools and Colleges.* Washington, DC: National Foreign Language Center.

GETTING LEARNERS ON THE WAY

Charles J. Quinn, Jr.

> Lost tourist: "How do you get to Carnegie Hall?"
> Elderly New Yorker: "Carnegie Hall? Practice!"

The identification of goals, or intended outcomes, along with the identification of means for judging when someone has reached them, are at the heart of any enterprise that aims to inculcate skills. Japanese language pedagogy is no exception. Furthermore, if these are the essential parameters of skill development, part of their essence is that they are interdependent. A goal that is a skill cannot be defined save in reference to some demonstrable and observable form. And so long as the starting point and goal are not coterminous, reaching that goal is necessarily the outcome of a developmental process. However, we may disagree about which goals should be pursued, in which order, and with which relative weightings, or materials. Constraints at this level apply to us all, so long as we claim new skills as the intended outcome of our pedagogy. Indeed, the most significant change in foreign language pedagogy over the last ten years is probably just this, the idea that demonstrable skills are a proper goal for instruction.

In the process, it has also become clear that taking identifiable skills as the avowed goals of instruction was a bit like opening Pandora's Box. The complexity with which communicative skills can be manifested, interrelated, and linked to further such skills down the road is daunting. There is, for example, a growing awareness that attempting to assess "oral proficiency" without reference to cultural fit is not very useful, insofar as competence in communicating is what we want to assess. So long as language skills are defined in relation to social life, in the activities of communication and thought, then we language pedagogues must come to terms with this complexity. If we would develop culturally viable communication skills, our instruction must aim well beyond an ability to render in the target language "meanings" that make sense in the base language. Nor is this need in any way cancelled simply because foreign language pedagogy can help inculcate the ability to communicate without at present being able to say, logically or biologically, exactly how or why this happens. We remain largely unable to explain why what we can help to make happen *has to* happen, but evidence seems to be mounting that, biologically speaking, a skill develops as neurophysiological responses to experience become changes of a neuroanatomical sort—such that, within limits chemical and temporal, what is "run" on our "wetware" ends up altering its configurations. But that is a story with its own daunting layers of complexity, and certainly not a topic to which I can do justice in this essay.

Regardless of how it happens or why it has to happen, however, there remains much to do to improve the efficiency of instructional practice. I would like to identify some of what the learner brings to the instructional process and variables that can be altered to improve the outcomes of that process. As innovations to a curriculum or syllabus, they may seem, on the face of it, simple, but since they aim to change assumptions that are culturally established, their efficacy depends on their being well integrated into the training, on more than one level and in several modalities. The challenge for us lies in adjusting the learning environment in ways that allow what will at first be quite foreign ideas to become common sense to the learners. In other words, we facilitate the growth of new culture—ways of thinking about and acting on learning Japanese—in place of culture that is variously problematic.

In what follows, I assume that the long-term goals of university training in Japanese are culturally viable communicative skills in the language as it is spoken and written today. There are other possible goals that can also be defined performatively, but what I have in mind can be summed up in the deceptively simple phrase "culturally comfortable communication" ("c³" if you like). This refers to a capacity to communicate with Japanese people who don't deal regularly with foreigners, as well as with those who do, in ways that do not require of those Japanese too much adaptation in understanding or making themselves understood—the kind of communicative experience that leaves the native feeling open to further encounters with that person.

For the foreign communicator in Japanese, then, interacting with a Japanese in ways that meet and leave him or her in a culturally comfortable way, entails quite a bit, from readily comprehended and comprehensible phonology (or orthography) to a sense of when and where to play which role — nothing less than a rhetorically competent, performatively integrated know-how of language as culture. I don't think this goal is too high, provided we understand it as a goal located *outside* the language program, which the language program's component courses are all directed toward. Given the degree to which communication in Japanese differs from communication in the learner's base language (English, for the most part), and given U.S. college curricula (five class sessions a week), it is a fact of life that a c3 that is rhetorically effective in a wide variety of contexts will in most cases emerge only some time after the learner has left the four-year language program. At the same time, however, we can provide instruction that develops a limited kind of c3, one which does not compromise in terms of the relevant phonological, orthographic, lexical or grammatical parameters, but which does involve a smaller set of context types and conversational moves. This is probably the best, if not the only, way to get a learner expecting and believing that s/he can develop culturally authentic communication skills—by making every lesson, from the lowest level on, an experience in recognizing and negotiating situations, roles, and moves that are recognizably Japanese (genre-wise, grammatically, lexically, phonologically, and orthographically).

In order to get the learner truly engaged in the training process, however, s/he needs to know what is at stake: what are the goals, long-term and short (as short as the next class hour)? What rationale motivates each part of the training process by linking it to those goals? Other teachers more experienced (and famous) than the likes of me have attested to the supercharging effect on learning that an understanding of the training process can have. One of them is James "Doc" Counsilman, the longtime coach of swimming at Indiana University, and innovator in the technique (breaststroke technique, interval training for swimming, focused isotonic muscle training, among others) and technology (pool-bottom lane markers, the poolside lap clock, the isotonic weight table) of that sport. (For those of us who are disinclined to consider the opinions of coaches, Counsilman's Ph.D. was in physiology, not physical education.) Concerning the swimmer's understanding of the training process, Counsilman had the following to say (1977: 255):

> It is the coach's responsibility to see that his program provides the swimmers with a feeling of accomplishment, even of creativity. After a practice session in the pool, a workout in the exercise room, or a stroke lecture in the classroom, the swimmer should feel he has made progress towards a goal. *In this feeling of accomplishment, the coach must educate him concerning the theories of training.* This information about the physiology of training will stimulate him to work more conscientiously than if he is merely following orders. (quoted in Walton 1992: 87; emphasis added)

The value of providing this kind of information, at points where it is apt to be heard and absorbed as knowledge, is that it nudges the learner in the direction of becoming his or her own coach. When a learner understands what has *caused* an improvement you can see or hear, s/he is a step closer to being able to replicate such improvements him- or herself. And the more often s/he experiences this kind of epiphany, the more likely s/he is to get in the habit of noticing change and abducing its causes. Insofar as the goal of culturally comfortable communication is to be reached at a point outside our programs, it is necessary that we foreign language coaches send our charges off with this ability to carry on as their own best mentors.

Another famous teacher who knew the liberating value of this kind of reflexive understanding was Vince Lombardi, one of the most accomplished coaches in the history of U.S. professional football. Lombardi is perhaps remembered more as an inspirer than as a technician, but some of his closest associates and former players dispute this image. He "could communicate an idea to his players, explain it so that they understood it—not only how to execute it but why," so that the players were in effect invited to focus on technique with an eye to how its proper execution can open one to opportunities that arise in the flow of play (Flynn 1973, cited in Walton 1992: 15).

It is easy, in our concern to get to work in teaching our students Japanese, to rush past or fail to address these meta-instructional variables—the learner's understanding of, attitude toward, belief in, and personal commitment to the task at hand, both right now and for the long haul. But these meta-variables make all the difference in how effective the instruction that teachers provide can actually be. At the learner's end, such variables are tied to a complex of biographical experiences, which range from the economic to the affective and sociocultural, and have undeniable effects on learning, insofar as they help determine for the learner such matters as attitude, attention and effort. Together, these learner variables can be included under the cover term "learner's mindset." The reason designers and executors of instruction are well advised to take active steps to know their learners' mindsets is simple. To the extent that we can enlist the active engagement of our students in pursuing the goals we have chosen, our goals become theirs, and instruction becomes more efficacious. It is far easier to push someone up when they coordinate their actions with your own than it is when they sit there looking around anxiously to see what happens next. If we can also kindle in some a passionate intensity, so much the better, but it needs to be an informed intensity, and not just a feeling that "You're my *sensei,* I'm loyal, I'll do whatever you tell me."

A meta-level of instruction, which lays out and addresses the questions of where we are going together in this Japanese class (or course, or program), why, and how we are going to get there, is not equally necessary for every learner who enrolls in Japanese 101, but it is still a safe bet that most American undergraduates stand to benefit from such meta-instruction. Some will not hear it, others will embrace it, and still others will need to be convinced, but few will say "Oh yeah, of course." Furthermore, they will need to learn these things not just in declarative mode, but in an operationalized way as well, if they are to really get the message. In other words, they will need to be convinced that our goals for the next class, for this week, for this semester, and our materials, techniques, methods, and other procedures, are worth pursuing and using in the ways we recommend. This is why talk about how the training's goals are served by the materials, methods and techniques must be backed up in actual practice, day-in and day-out.

Like the larger self it is part of, a mindset is a cultural construction, the product of interaction with others, in particular places, times, and social relations. Of primary concern to us as foreign language educators are those facets of a student's mindset that relate to learning a foreign language. For our purposes, we may ask how a learner regards, first of all, the task of developing a skill, then aspects of communication and language in general, and finally learning a foreign language in particular. What does s/he believe it is to communicate in language? In a foreign language? How does s/he think one gets good at doing so? How does s/he feel about speaking with a genuinely foreign pronunciation? Also relevant are learners' beliefs and attitudes concerning school and how things are done there. Let us take these facets of a late twentieth century young American's foreign language mindset in turn, and consider how they help or hinder the task of developing a capacity for culturally comfortable communication (c^3) in Japanese.

Some ten years ago, there appeared in *Forbes*, the business magazine, an article touting foreign language instruction that "works," such as that offered at Dartmouth under the direction of Professor John Rassias. I have written elsewhere about this piece of reporting, but it is worth quoting from again. The article begins by asking "Want to learn another language in a hurry? In less than two weeks? You can if you act like a little kid again." The skills one will acquire include "finding an apartment, shopping, and talking business," and they can be yours in three weeks, if you pay Berlitz to deliver them to you. Another school will "make you proficient enough to speak, comprehend, and read newspapers and books in your new language" in ten days, for $3,800 in 1986 dollars. The reader is left to assume that these phrases refer to talking business and reading newspapers as we normally do. Indeed, for people who have not previously learned to do these things in a foreign language (that is, the most likely customers), that is about the only way these descriptions *can* be understood, since the way such people perform these activities in their mother tongue is their only point of reference. And culture? In Dartmouth's summer program, "the cultural underpinnings" of a foreign language are said to be explained to beginners in the very language they are starting to learn.

The irony of a hardheaded business magazine suggesting to its readers, as a kind of "hot tip," that they should consider investing their money (considerable) and time (not much) in such "get proficient quick" schemes is delicious, if sobering. Imagine the consequences for *Forbes*' reputation if it were to advise buying stock that promised, say, to triple its price in two weeks. There are too many *Forbes* readers (including its writers and editors, one hopes) who know that these things generally do not happen in two weeks (unless of course someone drives the price of the stock up by circulating just such rumors). The fact that *Forbes* actually published this article suggests that, in the judgment of the editors, there are few potential readers in the United States who would take these claims at less than face value. That of course includes the students who fill our Japanese language classes. Behind the author's and the editors' tacit endorsement of these claims of "two weeks to talking business" is, I think, something like the following: if you can encode some content in foreign words, and have someone recognize that content, you are communicating in that language. We will return to this assumption—which most Americans seem to share—and what is problematic about it. But to contextualize it better, let us first consider the culture that nurtures the kind of readers' mindset assumed by the article in *Forbes*. If claims to instant prowess, put forward with breathtaking blitheness, sound somehow familiar to you, you are not alone. George Leonard (1991) has described this quintessentially American phenomenon as follows.

> Keep watching [television], and an underlying pattern will emerge. About half of the commercials, whatever the subject matter, are based on a climactic moment: The cake has already been baked; the family and guests, their faces all aglow, are gathered around to watch an adorable three-year-old blow out the candles. The race is run and won; beautiful young people jump up and down in ecstasy as they reach for frosted cans of diet cola. Men are shown working at their jobs for all of a second and a half, then it's Miller time. Life at its best, these commercials teach, is an endless series of climactic moments.
>
> And the sitcoms and soaps, the crime shows, and MTV all run on the same hyped-up schedule: (1) If you make smart-assed one-liners for a half hour, everything will work out fine in time for the closing commercials. (2) People are quite nasty, don't work hard, and get rich quickly. (3) No problem is so serious that it can't be resolved in the wink of an eye as soon as the gleaming barrel of a handgun appears. (4) The weirdest fantasy you can think of can be realized instantly and without effort. (29)

Leonard points these things out by way of describing what it is about late twentieth century American culture that is so inimical to the development of genuine, high level skills, the process he refers to as "mastery." What Leonard means by mastery is basically the practice of a 'way,' or *michi*. (If we momentarily strip the patina of age from this hallowed term, we notice that the word is indeed *michi* 'way, path, road,' and not *mokutekichi* 'destination, goal,' *shuuten* 'terminus,' or the like.) To develop a real proficiency at sports like tennis and *aikidoo* (examples from his own life), Leonard argues, one must be prepared, no matter how intently and regularly one practices, to endure extended periods when there is little or no visible advance in skill level—the plateau phenomenon. Like a number of successful coaches, such as Counsilman, Lombardi (both cited above), John Wooden (ten national basketball championships at UCLA), and Percy Cerutty (coaches of world record runners), not to mention systems engineer W. Edwards Deming, Leonard knows that to reach a desired outcome, you must focus not on the outcome, but on the process that leads to it. (As Deming would note, quality inspection of the *product* is too late.) And when the desired outcome is improvement in a complex skill, time frames are inevitably long.

The problem with the pattern described in the paragraphs quoted above is not so much the content, then, as it is the rhythm: "One epiphany follows another. One fantasy is crowded out by the next. Climax is piled upon climax. *There's no plateau*" (1991, 29). Leonard goes on to cite a variety of other examples of how happy outcomes and climaxes are presented as self-contained moments that spring out of "smart" decisions to buy this or that product (even if only for "fast, temporary relief"), and concludes that the American vision of the good life as "an endless series of climactic moments," the "quick-fix, anti-mastery mentality[,] touches almost everything in our lives" (1991, 33). This vision is not simply the invention of television: but "resonates in the rhetoric about scoring ("I don't care how you win, just win"), about effortless learning, instant celebrities, instant millionaires, and the 'number one' finger raised in the air when you score just once" (1991, 32-33). After reviewing American business and industry, including the rash of leveraged buyouts that made cultural heroes of corporate raiders, and the savings and loan crisis, Leonard (1991) warns that these are not unrelated phenomena, but related features of a coherent culture, or way of seeing and doing things.

> The same climate of thought that would lead some people to the promise that they can learn a new skill or lose weight without patient, long-term effort leads others to the promise of great riches without the production of value in return. (35)

If this strikes you as exaggerated alarmism, you might consider the extent to which current American prosperity rides on the back of a multi-trillion dollar deficit—a situation that has grown out of a mindset (read "culture") that refuses to mount any serious effort at growth and savings over the long term. In present-day America, "mastery, the path of patient, dedicated effort without attachment to immediate results" (1991, 37) is indeed at odds with much of what all of us see and hear every day.

You can probably guess the point I'm getting at. If a student sees a foreign language as something that can be bought from Berlitz, or "acquired" with the purchase of twenty credits of university coursework, s/he is very much in sync with the culture we live in. But she is also on a collision course with any training regimen that would develop a demonstrable capacity for nuanced communication in a foreign language. To the extent that our students have grown up into who they are in this culture—and their schooling seldom helps them here—they are little prepared for language courses that require daily practice and study, daily evaluation (e.g., evaluation of performance in class or of homework), and regular encounters with Life On the Plateau. Think of all the students in business, economics, and engineering who have time but for ten or fifteen credit hours of a foreign language the whole time they are in college. Even if such students are willing to invest the time and effort it takes to develop real skills in a foreign language, their major requirements often leave them time to take no more than the minimum. Nor is this limited to non-Japanese majors. There are American universities where Japanese language beyond a third level is not required for a Japanese major, and majors can take such upper level courses only as electives. There is seldom enough time in anyone's four-year curriculum for the kind of training that makes substantial progress toward c^3 skills.

Finally, recall the attrition rates that we see in all foreign language programs at the intermediate levels and beyond, but particularly in those of the truly foreign languages. Why should enrollments inevitably decrease as time spent in training increases? In Japanese, why is it that enrollment has grown so much in first or second year courses, but little beyond that—despite the fact that for professional use, you *must* proceed beyond the beginning levels? While language requirements that end with the elementary level and a lack of open time in a rigid curriculum are partly to blame, the influence of the larger culture's quick-fix mindset informs all of these. As many undergraduates will tell you, when it comes to getting a job, having some credits in "Japanese" (or "French" or "German") on your transcript is all that really matters. In the United States today this may actually be true, since if you can gain a basic competency in two or three weeks (as *Forbes* assures us), just imagine what two or three semesters will do. Who needs two years, much less three or four?

In a land where entire school districts routinely graduate students from high school who cannot read or do arithmetic at a sixth grade level (whatever that means), an unfamiliarity with training for demonstrable skills is hardly a problem unique to college language courses. Not that the skills deficit has gone unnoticed. In the rush to "outcome-based" education, many school districts and some universities have instituted "proficiency requirements" for certain subjects, such as math and language, mostly, it seems, to encourage students to study harder. The political appeal of "get tough" policies is undeniable, and in some cases the tougher exit requirements have been accompanied by curricular reform designed to get the learners to those outcomes in those time frames. But all too often, the exit requirements are put in place without creating any corresponding reform in curricula, without any retraining of teachers, without creating any incentives for reform among the very people who can do the most (parents and teachers) to make sure students achieve those goals. What happens? Too many students fail to measure up, and the new exit requirements have to be scrapped or lowered.

Focusing on exit requirements, to the exclusion of the processes that lead up to them and make them meetable at all, is yet another example of American culture's short-sighted obsession with the quick (preferably high-profile) fix. The problem we language pedagogues face in implementing curricula that develop demonstrable skills, then, is far larger than the individual learners who enroll in our classes. Their individual mindsets are but the products of a larger culture that everywhere legislates (and curricula set by school districts and universities *are* legislation) against investing the time and care that effect real change or learning. So, what to do? One thing seems clear. Unless we take active steps to familiarize our students with the nature of the task before us, provide them with conving rationales for the training they commit to, *and* lead them, through that training, to develop real skills, we are in effect doing just what those educators do who institute new exit requirements without taking steps to reform instruction.

Without changes in the way university language programs are administered (a question of governance), whatever we teachers might accomplish in training our students remains more or less limited. At the same time, however, improving the performance of a language program, in ways that can be documented in student performance, can be useful in *getting* the attention of administrators, particularly those who are themselves looking for ways to demonstrate that they have made a difference. This is a first step in involving them in support of our language programs. Noteworthy performance is attested, for example, when students are admitted to study abroad at higher levels, when they score well on standardized tests, win distinction in national competitions, and when they successfully apply their language skills in professional settings. So the best place to start is probably with the learners in one's courses. In the remainder of this paper, then, I'd like to focus on some particulars affecting learner understanding, awareness, and involvement in the training our programs provide.

There are a number of assumptions about what one learns in school and how it is done, including the teacher's role and the learner's role, that many American students beginning Japanese need to be guided in rethinking. This can be done declaratively, that is, by telling them, and it can also be shown, by demonstrating what's what over the course of the training regimen. Each modality, telling and showing, can accomplish something the other cannot, and when combined judiciously, each kind of message reinforces the other. We can explain to our students that their language teachers are not "cops," and that we do more than present models or dispense information. We can tell them to think of us more as coaches, who provide not only models, guided practice, explanations, and scrimmages (partially open-ended role play, with opportunities to create, not just react to, context), but also critical feedback through all of these interdependent activities. Such matters need to be explained, but once explained, it is crucial that students encounter them in action every day, so that they come to carry the models, advice, and other feedback around in their own heads, and have them at hand as they practice outside of class.

Careful explanation of their own role—what they need to be doing for themselves and how—is also useful, at the beginning of their training and intermittently over its course. Seemingly trivial procedures can, surprisingly enough, be unknown to the learner. What, for example, do you actually do with the audiotape for Lesson One? In what order? For how long? How do you watch and listen to a model dialog? We teachers need to remember the wisdom of *Syosin wasurubekarazu* 'Not to forget the beginner's mind[set].' One of my favorite examples of how important such things can be is what former UCLA basketball coach John Wooden had to say about socks.

> No basketball player is better than his feet. If they hurt, if his shoes don't fit, or if he has blisters, he can't play the game. It is amazing how few players know how to put on a pair of socks properly. I don't want blisters, so each year I give in minute detail a step-by-step demonstration as to precisely how I want them to put on their socks—every time. (1972: 106; quoted in Walton 1992: 53).

This tells us that John Wooden cared about detail, no matter how small. As you'd guess, the attention he paid to ensuring that his players understood how to put on their socks showed up in other aspects of his coaching as well.

But this kind of guidance needs to be put to the learners in an operationalized mode, too. We can talk all we want about the importance of studying video and audio tapes closely, and about learning how to hear what you've already learned in new contexts and new configurations by listening to new material several times before looking at its transcription. We can show them how to do this, and we can then insist on out-of-class rehearsal with both kinds of tapes, but unless the learners are also shown, every day, that doing so makes a difference in their performance, the advice will not ring true. For this reason, some evaluative feedback for every class hour, reported weekly, can be quite helpful. For most American undergraduates, daily feedback on one's performance in class will be another new idea that requires some explanation, if they are to go along with it. And again, its positive benefits will need to be demonstrated, not just described.

Evaluation, especially regular, daily evaluation, raises the question of anxiety, which can have a debilitating effect on performance. The kind of anxiety that arises when one cannot know or in any way control what happens to oneself is the worst kind. Regular evaluation of performance in class, however, should not and need not put the learner under this kind of negative stress. Here again, explanation-cum-demonstration can prove the point. If all in-class work is based on certain clearly defined out-of-class assignments, and if those assignments, when well executed, enable a highly evaluated performance in class, there is enough predictability to keep anxiety within reasonable bounds, for most people. Of course, if a language class is to be more than a rehash of homework, it must go beyond what was assigned for rehearsal and use it, along with other information, to lead the learners through the creation of something new.

This takes some getting used to, for until a learner has safely navigated such a class hour several times, s/he can't feel s/he is treading on firm ground. But it is right here, in getting used to the many ways in which a circumscribed set of homework assignments can open up into something new in class, that a learner comes to understand how model dialogs, response drills, and a knowledge of sociocultural constraints can help in coping with previously unencountered situations in Japanese. (Learning and acquisition are not the same thing, but that doesn't mean they are unrelatable.) The repeated experience of encountering a new, partially unpredictable situation, engaging it, and then coming up with a way to negotiate it, teaches that there is something to be gained, something new, from momentarily putting oneself at risk and then creating a way back to control. But critical feedback is necessary, most of all when the learner for some reason fails to find a way back.

Make no mistake about it, this is a very demanding kind of class to prepare for the teacher, too—a class where there is no dead time, where every activity retains a blend of cultural and linguistic naturalness, and where at the same time the "coach" retains the flexibility to explore promising detours as opportunities arise. A happy combination of anxiety-reducing predictability with the challenge of novelty makes for a class hour that leaves anyone who came prepared, including the instructor, feeling they have stretched for and reached something new. A poorly conceived combination can leave everyone disaffected, especially when a grade is riding on the performance. For regular evaluation of learner performance to work positively, a number of interrelated variables need to be handled adroitly: assignments for pre-class rehearsal must be clear and doable, the teacher must design and carry out a class hour that stretches the learners a little beyond what they rehearsed, evaluations must be consistent, and the learners need to feel they understand how all of this fits together. To put the matter mildly, this requires well-trained teachers who work hard and with imagination. GTAs new to the job, for example, will generally require close monitoring for a full academic term or more, on top of substantial pre-course training.

The more times a learner manages successfully to negotiate such classes, the less likely s/he is to be satisfied with anything less, and the less likely s/he is to be intimidated in future by new situations s/he encounters in Japanese. The more fully, too, s/he will understand what we mean when we describe the goals of this course, this semester, or this hour. Helping learners to develop this kind of stance toward learning to communicate in Japanese is a delicate business, and it takes time. Repeated success in handling controlled but partially open-ended situations, when combined with careful criticism of unsuccessful attempts (this makes the success believable), breeds confidence, as no premature, uncontrolled dive into "real" Japanese can. It is of course possible and quite useful to employ unadapted texts or tapes with a high percentage of unfamiliar language in class, so long as what is done with them is doable in ways familiar to the learners. Regular practice in dealing with pieces of largely opaque language can help build a "can do" attitude too, so long as the activity itself is carried out with language controlled by the learners.

This kind of confidence is a very useful direction for a language learner's mindset to grow in, but getting there only comes out of repeatedly putting oneself at risk, in performance that is partly open-ended. Our task as instructors is to make sure that those risks are always controlled enough so as to be challenging but manageable. For the pedagogical stance it develops in a learner, for the attitude it embodies, a language-learning mindset is one of the most basic things we can teach, since it will carry the learner well beyond us and our programs of instruction. All things equal, a student who is knowledgeable about the training process is more likely to be actively engaged in it, and looking for ways to adapt, instead of sitting and reacting—a far cry from a study in paralyzing anxiety.

I have left what is perhaps the most basic mindset issue for last, one that nevertheless needs addressing right from the start of instruction. This is the question of what it is to communicate in any language, and in a foreign language in particular. Most American undergraduates will probably assume, with the readership of *Forbes*, that a foreign language is, like one's own language, a body of words, grammatical patterns, sounds, and letters. They will also assume that the meanings are "in" the words, and, consequently, that learning to communicate in a foreign language is a matter of learning the foreign words (structures, sounds and letters) that carry the meanings one wants to communicate. Indeed, many foreign language teachers will tell you something similar—that the most important thing for our students to learn is how to express what they want to say.

Be that as it may, what learners of Japanese need to hear, and see demonstrated in culturally authentic models, is that it's not just the words that differ, it's the meanings, too. It is *not* up to a cultural American to decide what is felicitously said or sayable in a given situation in Japanese. Such matters have been decided in Japanese communities over their histories, and they are something a learner needs to see and hear at work before s/he can know the circles of their significance. Having done so, he can learn something useful from trying these moves and meanings out for her- or himself, in other situations. As Professor Watabe pointed out earlier, this principle informs so simple a choice as what to say when remarking on a handsome car—not *Ano kirei na kuruma o mite kudasai!* (the perfectly grammatical equivalent of 'Look at that good-looking car!'), but *Kirei na kuruma desu nee*! (literally 'It's a good-looking car, isn't it!'). For learners to learn to say "what they want to say" in Japanese, in ways that stand a good chance of making sense and working to their advantage, they need to watch and listen to people saying the kinds of things that are actually said, when they are said, to whom, and to what effect. Communication that is culturally comfortable requires a reliable feel for words, grammar, and sounds as they relate to all of these contexts—not only the propositional "who, what, when, where," but also the social where's and who's, and the epistemological (unfamiliar "news" vs. shared knowledge). The beginning learner needs to understand that Japanese is not just a funny way of speaking American, and that s/he is not being untrue to her- or himself when behaving in a coherently Japanese way; s/he is just communicating in another culture.

Actually, this is one more lesson a skills-based language course offers that is at the heart of a liberal education. The more immediately accessible part of the lesson is that meanings are made and remade from a fabric many others have worked many times, to many ends, and that those ends are what one starts with in one's own weavings. A somewhat more profound (and less accessible) part of the same lesson reveals itself as a learner approaches a capacity for c^3 and develops the ability to orient her- or himself to others in ways that differ radically from those s/he grew up with. An example of this would be developing a reliable feel for referring to oneself, other people, and information in terms of the indexical coordinates of *uchi* 'inside' and *soto* 'outside'. What comes with the habit of situating oneself, one's claims and one's questions with reference to such different anchor points? For one thing, a first-hand, experiential conviction that this way of living is just as real as the ways one grew up with. That's a profound lesson for any of us.

References

Bachnik, Jane M. and Charles J. Quinn, Jr., eds. 1994. *Situated Meaning: Inside and Outside in Japanese Self, Social Life, and Language.* Princeton: Princeton University Press.

Bagamery, Anne. 1984. "Scaling the ALPs," *Forbes*, September 24, 1984, 210-12.

Bruner, Jerome S. 1990. *Acts of Meaning.* Cambridge, MA: Harvard University Press.

Counsilman, James. 1977. *Competitive Swimming Manual for Coaches and Swimmers.* Bloomington, IN: Counsilman Co.

Deming, W. Edwards. 1986. *Out of the Crisis.* Cambridge, MA.: MIT Center for Advanced Engineering Study.

Edelman, Gerald M. 1992. *Bright Air, Brilliant Fire: On the Matter of the Mind.* New York: Basic Books.

Flynn, George, ed. 1973. *Vince Lombardi on Football.* New York: New York Graphics Society.

Gazzaniga, Michael S. 1992. *Nature's Mind.* New York: Basic Books.

Goody, Esther N., ed. 1995. *Social Intelligence and Interaction.* Cambridge: Cambridge University Press.

Kramer, Jerry. 1972. *Lombardi: Winning is the Only Thing.* New York: World Book.

Leonard, George. 1991. *Mastery.* New York: Dutton.

Walton, Gary M. 1992. *Beyond Winning: The Timeless Wisdom of the Great Philosopher Coaches.* Champaign, IL.: Leisure Press.

Wooden, John. 1972. *They Call Me Coach: As Told to Jack Tobin.* Waco, TX: Word Books.

JAPANESE LANGUAGE TEACHING WITHOUT TEACHING CONTEXT

"Are We Producing *Onti* Learners?"

Masakazu Watabe

With a few exceptions, Japanese language instruction in this country has followed the general trends of foreign language teaching (Watabe, 1994): *Grammar-Translation Approach* (University of California at Berkeley, 1900s; Harvard, Columbia,1930s), *Audio-lingual Approach* (Yale, 1940s), *Cognitive Approach* (1960s) and *Natural/Communicative/Proficiency Approach* (1980s), to name some major approaches of this century. Today the so-called Natural/Communicative/Proficiency approach has been spreading very rapidly and influencing many Japanese language teachers across the nation. Most of them directly apply the methods developed by linguists, Second-Language Acquisition researchers, and foreign language teachers of Indo-European languages and of English as a Second Language (See Tohsaku's Acknowledgments, for example.) Although some of the recent proposals and findings across different languages seem to be very promising, I still wonder whether the methods and approaches developed for students learning languages of the same family can be directly applied to the teaching of a foreign language not related at all, such as Japanese. Similarly, should general methods and approaches be incorporated and applied in the same way to teaching different levels of students and different language skills?

It is true that certain claims should apply across the board since we are dealing with the human language learning process; however, we must not apply them blindly without considering what I call "the context of language teaching." The context of language teaching includes things such as (1) the native language background of the learners; (2) teaching Japanese as a second language vs. as a foreign language; (3) teaching different skills, i.e. speaking, reading, listening, and writing; (4) teaching at different levels, beginning, intermediate and advanced; (5) teaching intensive vs. teaching a one hour a day course; (6) the learner's age and background, etc. It is ironic that though the current approach emphasizes the importance of teaching language in context (Hadley 1993), with which I totally agree, few have looked at different teaching contexts.

I would like to narrow the focus of my discussion to Japanese language teaching at the college level to native speakers of English and examine some of the techniques and hypotheses widely claimed and used in the most recent movement: the natural/ communicative/proficiency approach to teaching Japanese. The questions I would like to ask are: Is it more effective and powerful than the other methods and approaches that have come and gone? Should it be applied to Japanese language teaching regardless of the teaching context? In other words, do these principles now claimed by the natural/ communicative/ proficiency advocators apply to all the levels, to all four skills, to different teaching environments?

My experiences and my examination of learners' profiles at my own institution and at nationwide programs such as the Middlebury Japanese School and the East Asian Summer Language Institute at Indiana University, reveal that those who have had the natural/communicative/proficiency approach of Japanese instruction, experiences, and materials at the earlier levels of language studies tend to develop what I call "linguistic *onti*" in learning a foreign language. They are learners that develop very inaccurate interlanguage, or in some cases, fossilization (Selinker 1974; Selinker and Lamendella 1979); and although they become very comfortable with their abilities to communicate, they are insensitive to the basic characteristics of the Japanese language and culture. They are those who are very fluent, but constantly use wrong particles, cannot distinguish words of different classes such as Adjectivals, na-Nominals, and Nominals with the appropriate conjugations, especially in embedded clauses. Their problems are not just in morpho-syntactic inaccuracies, but in other areas such as supersegmental problems of interchanging the Japanese mora system with the English syllable system, or pitch accent with the primary and secondary stress system. They also exhibit little concept of pragmatic and sociolinguistic principles of Japanese. I am sure many of you have had some experiences with these students. They are students who would respond to the teacher with phrases such as: *"Arigatoo."* and *"Ohayoo."* One of the most unforgettable occasions of this sort occurred after a speech in Japanese given by a consulate general of Japan to the students on our campus. One of our students who learned Japanese through exposure to the language in Japan came up to the consulate general afterwards and said: *"XXX-san, anata no hanasi, totemo yokatta yo."* I still remember the perplexed look on the consulate general's face, not knowing how to react to the student's compliment. I do not think the student ever realized what kind of mixed message he was giving with his intended compliment. This anecdotal incident aside, however, the students' most serious problem is that they usually cannot correct their own mistakes as well as students who have gone through more rigorous drills, exercises and explanations of the language at the early stage of learning. Many of them, especially those who acquired the language through total exposure with natives in Japan, can manage most of the tasks, functions, and situations of advanced and superior levels of the Oral Proficiency Interview standards and are very loquacious and fluent; yet, their Japanese tends to be inaccurate, and it indicates strong traces of direct transferring of concepts from English.

These problems are very common among students who acquired language skills through exposure to the language, and I am afraid that the current stress on the natural/communicative/proficiency approach, especially in the early stages of language instruction, will produce inaccurate and inappropriate outcomes. In particular, practice like the following at the beginning level in developing oral skills is bound to produce this type of speaker in a lifelong learning process:

> Opportunities must be provided for active communicative interaction among students. The use of small-group and paired communicative practice has several advantages in building oral proficiency (Hadley 1993, 250). Group work encourages interaction and communication. For this reason, this textbook includes a variety of pair work, small-group work, and interviews, during which students can practice using language on a stress-free, nonthreatening atmosphere (Tohsaku 1994, xix)

In fact, the advocators of the Natural/Communicative/ Proficiency approach remind us that many educational researchers have proven that peer learning is effective and not limited to foreign language learning (Tohsaku 1993). But it is precisely because of this fact that we should avoid, as much as possible, group activities before the students internalize pronunciation and the major structural frame of the Japanese language. Group activities, especially without model input early in language learning, will foster internalization of inaccurate output.

The corollary to the lack of a model speaker in too many group activities in the communicative approach is an over- (and maybe too early) emphasis on communication and function before the learners internalize and are able to use the structural frame of the target language. Look at the two major hypotheses proposed by Hadley (1993) for developing oral proficiency:

Hypothesis 1: Opportunities must be provided for students to practice using language in a range of contexts likely to be encountered in the target culture. (238-266)
Hypothesis 2: Opportunities should be provided for students to practice carrying out a range of functions (tasks) likely to be necessary in dealing with others in the target culture.
Corollary 3: Creative language practice (as opposed to exclusively manipulative or convergent practice) must be encouraged in the proficiency oriented classroom. (261)

These might work very well in teaching Indo-European languages where analogous structures from English might be a strong tool and strategy. However, in teaching Japanese these kinds of creative practices must not be recommended before the students have learned and internalized appropriate structural patterns and vocabulary they can use in different situations. Otherwise, the students do not have the means in their minds to communicate, and they tend to rely on their knowledge of English structures and transfer it to the Japanese language with a one-on-one vocabulary translation from English. These sentences, without being corrected in a so-called "stress free atmosphere," will become a part of their interlanguage system, which is extremely difficult to correct later on in their language learning process, resulting in what Jorden would call "abominable fluency." We must not foster translation, but rather focus our attention on helping the students develop the Japanese language system in their minds. We must help them establish the habit of expressing their ideas within the structural knowledge of the target language they have learned, rather than encouraging them to communicate haphazardly with all the means they have available, including the knowledge of the base language, strategies of human communication, etc. In other words, our focus of instruction and methodology, especially at the early stage, should be to teach and help students internalize the basic Japanese language system and to help them avoid transferring and translating from English to Japanese. The creativity in production we should foster in the early stages of language study should not be a free access to the learner's knowledge and strategy; instead, it should be the ability and strategy of the learner to express ideas within the Japanese structures and vocabulary he/she knows how to use. Our efforts should be to teach structures and provide the natural contexts in which the different structures they have learned can be used. This requires a great deal of training, practice, and preparation on the part of the instructor because the instructor must think of natural situations and contexts in which a certain sentence structure to be practiced is called for.

Needless to say, at this early stage, as the students try to produce a sentence within the structure they have been learning, their mistakes, inaccuracies, unnative-like expressions and behaviors must be pointed out and corrected directly or indirectly. Of course, the teacher must not make corrections to provoke or discourage the students; however, the students need feedback from the teacher in order to refine their language skills and bring them as close as possible to native competence. In fact, if the drills and exercises are limited to the sentence structures and vocabulary that they have already studied, the students usually can correct their own mistakes with a short cue from their instructor. If the learner does not realize what is acceptable and not acceptable, he/she will have a difficult time refining and defining the language system he/she is trying to learn. We must not encourage methods and approaches that do not enable the students to be sensitive to inaccurate or inappropriate language. By helping the student cultivate this sensitivity for hypothesizing and refining his/her understanding of the system, we help the students to become independent language learners. The current natural/communicative/proficiency oriented approach seems to dull this sensitivity in the name of "communication and a stress-free atmosphere."

However, I am not saying that the natural/communicative/ proficiency approach is totally bad or wrong. As I mentioned at the very beginning, the merits of a certain method and approach must be weighed and examined with respect to the teaching context. In my opinion, the communicative approach is excellent after the basic accurate structure, vocabulary, pronunciation, and sociolinguistic factors have been internalized by the learners. In other words, it is useful and effective only after two or three years of more rigid and systematically programmed instruction. It might also be effective in developing reading and listening skills. But it should never be employed at the beginning level, especially in developing oral skills. With these arguments against the current natural/communicative/ proficiency approach and learning Japanese as a lifelong process in mind, I would like to propose a model for Japanese language instruction at the college level. The most reasonable and practical curriculum design that I have yet seen for the Japanese language is the one proposed by Galal Walker for his Chinese program at EASLI in Indiana. A slight modification and the application of his ideas to a lifelong language learning process will produce something like the diagram model in Figure 1.

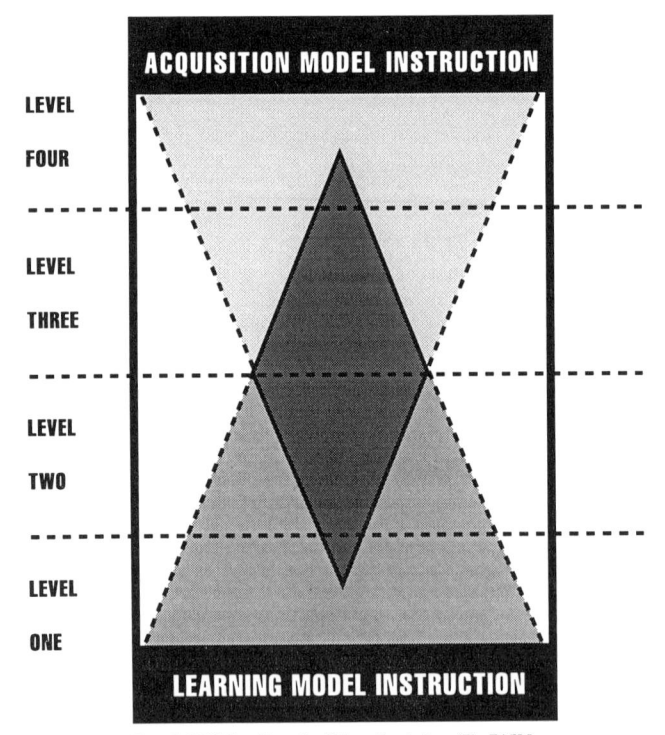

From Galal Walker "Intensive Chinese Curriculum: (The EASLI Model" JCLTA, Volume XXIV: No. 2, May 1989, p. 49)

Figure 1

Learning model instruction represents instructor-oriented language instruction in which the structure, drills, and vocabulary are strongly controlled by the instructor. As the students advance in the language, this control becomes less and less and the students increasingly become independent learners of the language. Of course, learners are not expected to know all there is to know about the language by the time they graduate from college, but at least they should have enough basics, skills, and strategies to be independent learners. The inverted triangle, Acquisition Model Instruction, represents the independent learner's attempt to acquire the language natively through practicing and applying the skills that have been learned through truly authentic materials and without the assistance of formal language instruction.

In this model, the basic structural patterns should be covered in the first two years. It should be noted also that the curriculum in these two levels should be syntactically oriented rather than having a functional, notional, natural orientation. Of course, the structures must not be taught without the context or without showing how they are to be used in the natural context. However, in order for the structures to be internalized correctly at this stage, the introduction of the forms must be controlled. As Quinn (1991) strongly and aptly argued in reviewing *Japanese: The Spoken Language*, this type of controlled syntactic-based approach is much more powerful than a curriculum built from highly specific whole situations or functions.

Take, for example, the notion or function of request and command forms in Japanese. Even with one verb, *miru*, you could say *miro, mite, minasai, goran, goran nasai, mite kudasai, mite itadakemasu ka, mite kudasaimasen ka, mite itadakemasen ka, goran kudasaimasen ka*. Rather than organizing the materials, activities, and exercises around the different situations using these forms, it makes more sense to structure the instruction from the uniformity of the forms and teach how the forms are used in different situations. In teaching other Indo-European languages, some syntactic parallelism from English may apply with a little modification in the target language. But the Japanese system and situation is too different. It deals with command form, -te form, usage of negation, question, the concepts of honorifics, deistic verbs of giving and receiving, potential forms and level of speech. Without going over these concepts one by one and making sure that the learners are internalizing the forms and how to use them in different situations in well-conceived and structured yet natural drills and exercises, again leaves students with transfer strategies or inaccurate and vague notions and means of communication.

Quinn also masterfully argues the importance of effective drills, considered by many foreign language teachers today an obsolete practice. He suggested that the learning of subskills before operating on the global scale is necessary not only in foreign language education, but also in sports, performing arts, and problem-solving disciplines such as chemistry. I could not agree with him more, and I will not elaborate on this topic further, except to point out that with the development of technology, computers can help immensely to assist students in doing meaningful drills with native informants on the computer. Computer drills are much more effective than texts or even tapes because of the random ordering capabilities, availabilities of visual cues and model native responses. It is unfortunate that computers are being used to produce fancy and elaborate programs that are not pedagogically sound. I believe it is because of the negative opinion of drills in the communicative movement of language teaching that very few people are developing simple yet effective computer aided drills. Instead, a lot of effort and money is being spent on projects that usually do not help the students internalize the basic structures of the language.

Computers cannot and should not be a replacement for the human teacher or a textbook; rather, they should be used to enhance and supplement the teacher and the textbook. We must not spend precious resources in developing computer materials that a teacher and a written text can do better or as well. Instead, let the computers be used to do more repetitive drills and exercises that will help students internalize the basic structural framework in the target language, or in the advanced level for more recognition practices. If I extend Quinn's analogy of sports, computers can be a tennis ball or baseball machine that can throw balls at you to practice and develop your basic form, subskills that will be helpful in playing a real game later.

Another important concept to remember in the first two years of basic instruction in Japanese is to stress the spoken language. Although it is very important for adult learners to learn the written language as soon as possible, the written text is a slow way to teach students to internalize the basic structures of the language. Furthermore, dependence on written materials in the early stages will hamper oral fluency, whereas mastering basic structures orally will not hamper reading fluency as students progress onto the written language. I would not oppose introducing written symbols and sentences of vocabulary and structures as soon as they have been internalized orally, but to try to teach basic structures from written materials needs to be avoided because it reduces the speed, spontaneity, and fluency of the learner and hampers his/her internalization of the basic structure.

Teaching Japanese is a function of at least three elements, usually demonstrated in the students' outcome: accuracy, fluency, and affectedness. Accuracy includes the accuracy of pronunciation with native-like intonation, native-like structural accuracy in oral or written production, and native-like understanding of both oral and written materials. It requires phonetic, morpho-syntactic, sociolinguistic, and pragmatic accuracy in the target language. Fluency deals with the speed at which communication is processed. It includes native-like spontaneity in performing tasks dealing with productive or receptive skills in both oral and written materials. One of the seemingly neglected challenges in language learning is that communication involves speed and natives have skills to process communication at a certain speed. It requires spontaneity, vocabulary, and the means to get the message across with native-like speed. Affectedness encompasses all the psychological conditions of the learner. We are not teaching robots or computers, but we are teaching humans to learn the language. We cannot disregard the psychological state or affectedness of the adult learner, such as how motivated s/he becomes as s/he continues the study of the language; what her/his language aptitude for a non-Indo-European language might be; what her/his style of learning is; or any other factors that a learner (an adult human) will bring to the classroom. Figure 2 is a graphic representation of the function of these three elements.

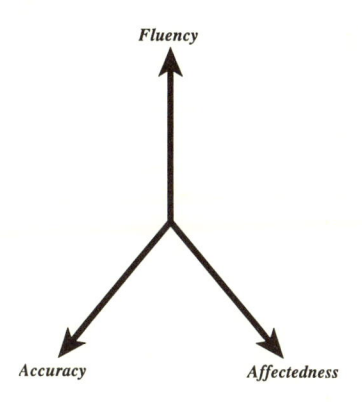

Figure 2

Ideally, the approach should be such that all three factors of outcome will be enhanced and increased simultaneously; however, due to time constraints and the fact that we are dealing with adult second language learning, one has to consider trade-offs. *A Framework for Introductory Japanese Language Curricula in American High Schools and Colleges* talks about the trade-offs of classroom time (Unger et al. 1993, 13). This trade-off concept, however, applies to a far wider range of teaching. The emphasis on structural accuracy may reduce students' performance in fluency or affectedness. In other words, one hour of instruction about the target language in the native language may increase the accuracy of the students, but reduce the actual practice time of fluency in the target language. The constant correction of the students' performance may help them become more accurate in their pronunciation, but some students' motivation for learning may be affected. With the current natural/communicative/ proficiency approach, the tendency and emphasis seem to have gravitated more toward affectedness and fluency at the sacrifice of accuracy. My contention is that during the first two years of college instruction, especially in oral production, the emphasis should be more towards accuracy. In fact, accuracy may not be something that should be measured in degree as the proficiency guidelines may suggest, but rather, teaching should be a progression from learning a small number of accurate expressions and structures to developing a repertoire of accurate expressions and structures. Once the basic foundation of the language is internalized by learners accurately, then more free and less contrived, controlled, and structured natural/communicative/ proficiency activities including study abroad, content-based instruction, courses for special purposes, etc. can be recommended, but not before.

References

Hadley, Alice Omaggio. 1993. *Teaching Language in Context.* Boston: Heinle and Heinle Publishers.

Quinn, Charles. 1991. "Giving Spoken Language Its Due," *JATJ* 25(2): 224-267.

Selinkler, Larry. 1974. "Interlanguage." In *New Frontiers in Second Language Learning.* Eds. J. Schumann and N. Stenson, 114-136. Rowley, MA: Newbury House.

——— and John T. Lamendella. 1979. "The Role of Extrinsic Feedback in Interlanguage Fossilization.," Language Learning 29: 363-375.

Tohsaku, Yasu-Hiko. 1994. *Yookoso! An Invitation to Contemporary Japanese*. New York: McGraw-Hill.

Unger, J. Marshall, Fred Lorish, Mari Noda, and Yasuko Wada. 1993. *A Framework for Introductory Japanese Language Curricula in American High Schools and Colleges*. Washington D.C.: The National Foreign Language Center.

Walker, Galal. 1989. "Intensive Chinese Curriculum: The EASLI Model," *JCLTA* 24(2): 43-83.

Watabe, Masakazu. 1994. "Amerika ni okeru Nihongo Kyooiku no Genzyoo—Kyoozyuhoo kara no Koosatu." ("The Present State of Japanese Language Education in the United States: Observations from Pedagogy") Presented at The Hokkaido University. March, 1994.